Outwitting Ants

Outwitting Ants

101 Truly Ingenious Methods and Proven Techniques to Prevent Ants from Devouring Your Garden and Destroying Your Home

Cheryl Kimball

With illustrations by Linda Isaacson

Series Concept Created by Bill Adler, Jr.

The Lyons Press
Guilford, CT
The Lyons Press is an imprint of The Globe Pequot Press

The Lyons Press is an imprint of The Globe Pequot Press.

Printed in the United States of America

10 9 8 7 6 5 4 3 2 1

Library of Congress Cataloging-in-Publication Data

Kimball, Cheryl.
  Outwitting ants : 101 truly ingenious methods and proven techniques to prevent ants from devouring your garden and destroying your home / Cheryl Kimball ; with illustrations by Linda Isaacson.
      p. cm. – (Outwitting series)
  ISBN 1-58574-549-9 (pbk. : alk. paper)
  1. Ants–Control. I. Title. II. Series.
  SB945.A4K55 2003
  632'.796–dc21
                        2002154423

To my father, Walter Kimball, who died the fall that I was writing this book. I could chatter on about anything, including ants, and he would listen in apparent fascination.

Contents

Acknowledgments

Thanks first to Linda Isaacson who took on the project of illustrating this book with the same enthusiasm that she takes on everything else. Her artwork, good humor, sincerity, and fascination with all life have enhanced my own life for the many years of our friendship.

Thanks also to Orkin Exterminating Company, Inc., in particular Jennifer McDuffee, formerly of Orkin's publicity department, who was prompt and helpful; as well as Frank Meek, of Orkin Technical Services, who sent me photographs, cheerfully answered my questions, and makes outwitting ants a fascinating topic.

Thanks also to all of my family and friends who looked at me only a *little* strangely when I told them what I was writing about these days.

Outwitting
Ants

Introduction

"In the past, ants for me were small, feisty insects that went on all my picnics. Never again will I step on an ant."

—Robert F. Sisson, "At Home with the Bulldog Ant"

M r. Sisson's fascinating firsthand study and resulting photojournalism in *National Geographic* make it clear how one could become so enamored of ants. Before taking on this book project, I already went out of my way to avoid harming animals of any kind, but the more I learned about ants the more I wondered how I would ever be able to walk on the ground again for fear of killing one of these hard-working creatures. Artist and illustrator of this book, Linda Isaacson, was also captivated and would tell me about her latest ant drawing, exclaiming, "She's so sweet!" Linda implored me to not spend a lot of time in the book explaining how to kill them. Ants have a way of getting to you.

Throughout my research I came across sentiments by other casual ant aficionados that mirrored Mr. Sisson's opening quotation above. "The more you study ants, the more compulsive it becomes, and you begin to envy their efficient, seemingly utopian way of life," Joshua Tompkins writes in a great *Los Angeles Times Magazine* piece, "Empire of the Ants."

That said, ant research also serves to make most writers less enamored of the ant in close proximity, including Mr. Tompkins, who reaches the conclusion that, although ant life may

1

look utopian at first glance, "you see them getting their heads torn off by a bunch of other ants and you think twice." The more I read, the more it became clear that these innocent-looking little insects can not only be destructive but they also carry disease, so I wound up this book project less tolerant of them scurrying around on my kitchen counters. I admire a lot of animals, but that doesn't mean I want them all living in my house. And anyone who has ever lived in a house besieged knows that keeping ants at bay is a constant process.

Whenever I admitted that I was working on a book about outwitting ants, the person to whom I was speaking invariably regaled me with his or her personal ant story, usually of the carpenter ant invasion kind. Others would relate the details we've all come to know about ants—that they can carry many times their own weight, that the males die shortly after mating with the queen, and so on. Common ant stories revolved around painful encounters with fire ants or having an "ant farm" as a child.

Many years ago I had my first real encounter with the industriousness of the ant. Returning from a long weekend away, I settled into bed ready to rest up for the coming workweek. In the quiet of the darkened bedroom I heard a crunching sound. Assuming it was a mouse, I turned on a light, got a rough idea of where the noise was coming from, rapped on the wall a couple of times to encourage the mouse to move on, and went back to bed. The crunching didn't skip a beat. Lights on, lights off, rapping on walls, stomping feet—nothing seemed to deter this mouse. Finally, I moved to the living room sofa and called my landlord in the morning.

Vastly more experienced in the interactions of homes and pests than I, my landlord quickly determined that the noise was being caused by an infestation of carpenter ants. He called an extermination service and a woman in coveralls with a stethoscope draped over her neck snooped around my little house. She confirmed his diagnosis and figured out that the carpenter ants had made their way in from underneath, tunneled through the floor and, with the luck of the *Hogan's Heroes* team, broke through directly below a sliding hollow door tucked into the wall that always stayed in the open position. When they got to the bottom of the door they just kept going straight up, constructing their colony inside the door. The exterminator, who repeated the phrase "dagnabbit" numerous times, listened with her stethoscope and showed us how high the colony had managed to get. She was so excited, she begged my landlord to let her have the door. Go for it lady . . .

That was the last memorable encounter I had with ants until a few years later when I became a homeowner myself. The now-unmistakable crunching sound once again kept me awake one night. A little pile of sawdust accumulated on the kitchen counter from the carpentry work I assumed was going on above. Ring, ring, comes the exterminator. Bye, bye carpenter ants.

I try to follow all the suggested preventative measures, avoiding the open invitations to colonize my home. I look with disdain at firewood piled within ten feet of a building. I sweep crumbs off of counters and keep sweets in plastic burpable containers and wipe clean the bottle of olive oil after each use. While shen-ant-igans may be taking place in the dark recesses of my house's superstructure, no crunching has kept me up at night lately.

I now rank among those who have outwitted at least one ant so far in my lifetime. After you read this book, you'll be prepared to outwit your first ant too.

The History and Folklore of the Ant

"Go to the ant, thou sluggard. Consider her ways and be wise: which having no guide, overseer or ruler, provideth her meat in the summer and gathereth her food in the harvest."
—Proverbs 6:6–8

The story of the ant begins in the Mesozoic era, approximately 100 to 120 million years ago. The ant is assumed to have derived from a creature similar to that ancient and ubiquitous of all insects, the cockroach, who showed up on earth somewhere between 400 and 250 million years ago. The termite has been around twice as long as the ant, appearing in the Jurassic or early Cretaceous Period, around 200 million years ago.

"In the very earliest of Tertiary times, separated from our day by fifty million years or more, the social life of ants had almost ceased evolving, and their final physical form almost fixed," scientist Caryl P. Haskins notes in his 1939 work, *Of Ants and Men*.[1] Only slight tweakings occurred from that time forward.

Ants are perhaps the most colonially organized of all insects. Yet curiously, it took insects several million years of existence before coming to understand the benefits of colonization to creatures their size. And some insects still fail to take advantage of colonies. But not ants—their intricate use of them for survival makes our own Plymouth Rock colony seem like an evolutionary step backward in species development.

Ant Evidence

Ants have left abundant testimony of their long history. As Haskins points out, "fossil records are available which are so complete and beautiful that wandering worker ants which were trapped in the sticky resin of the ancient Samlandic black conifer forests of Germany and Central Europe two million years ago are more perfectly preserved for us today than are the sentries of Pompeii and Herculaneum."[2]

In the 1960s, the New Jersey shore provided some of the oldest fossils preserved in amber, dating back ninety million years when dinosaurs were king. Others were soon found around the world: perfectly preserved specimens of what we now call ants.

These fossil records give scientists a clear picture of the ant's evolution, allowing for a more thoroughly studied evolutionary history than most other animal species—including our own. We know more about the ant's development than we may ever know about ours.

> Around 2,000 years ago, the Roman naturalist Pliny believed that a giant ant "the color of a cat and as large as an Egyptian wolf mined gold in the mountains north of India."[3]

Ant life began in the time of the dinosaurs. They evolved from the parasitic members of the order Hymenoptera, which take form today as the ichneumon flies. Ants, however, were more directly descended from a parasitic group of wasps; this group is considered to be a more intelligent life form because they took on the responsibility of protecting their eggs and parenting their young instead of merely laying eggs and leaving their survival to fate. A primitive antlike family of Hymenoptera known as Scoliidae, recognized as the beginning of the true ant, is still in existence today, almost a living fossil.

The physical evolution of the ant included the quicker development of female offspring and the isolation and immobility of the reproducing queen. As ants evolved physically, basic habits evolved as well. Even changes in food preferences took place, shifting from an exclusively carnivorous diet to a wider-ranging one, including the ant foodstuffs we know today—honey, seeds, and other plant materials—making survival not only easier but also more likely. They expanded their selection of nesting sites, moving from the sole use of soil-built nests to building nests made of their own paper creation in trees and shrubs.

The development of a stable colony structure soon followed, "culminating in the remarkably complex organizations of ants of the present time."[4] Eventually, ants diverged into three subfamilies:

- **Myrmicinae** retained the stinging capability of their wasp forebears and have agricultural habits.
- **Formicae** replaced the stinger with formic acid glands, and are the most dominant of ant types today.
- **Dolichoderinae** is a less dominant group, of which Argentine ants are the most prevalent.

Ant R Us

Ants, their societies, and their behavior have long been compared to and contrasted against an unlikely counterpart: humans. Haskins, in *Of Ants and Men*, posed probing questions regarding this link:

> Are there any real parallels to be drawn between the societies of ants and men? To what extent can we "hu-

manize" ant societies without falling into the criminal error of hopeless anthropomorphism? . . . Have ants, by virtue of their enormously great antiquity as social animals, gained more social wisdom than we humans, and have they fallen into and rectified social errors which we have not yet committed, or have only begun to commit?[5]

For every one person in this world, there are one million ants!

Pest Ants in the U.S.

North America came equipped with plenty of indigenous ants that have proven to be plenty pesty to humans. But some pest ants came to the United States via accidental importation.

A common way for many things to sneak beyond home borders—intentionally or not—is by ship. Ships once used soil for ballast and any ant that found itself in that soil went along for the ride. Although two species of fire ants are considered native to North America, the two imported species—the black imported fire ant, *Solenopsis richteri*, and the red imported fire ant, *Solenopsis invicta*—were first spotted in Alabama, probably having arrived via cargo ship from South America in the early part of the twentieth century.

The imported ants found agreeable conditions in North America and by 1953 they had invaded 102 counties in ten states. Researcher Timothy C. Lockley notes that "today, the red imported fire ant has spread throughout the southeastern U.S. and Puerto Rico replacing the two native species and displacing the black imported fire ant."[6]

Argentine ants swashbuckled into the South, too. First noticed on the docks in New Orleans in 1891, they wiped out native ants as well as competing pests, such as chiggers and bedbugs. They also damaged the cut flower industry, however, and southern sugar farmers had to fight to save their crops. The Argentine ant migrated to southern California at the turn of the twentieth century and took a brief one hundred years—barely a catnap in ant evolution—to become that state's most harmful pest.[7]

A statistic commonly recounted in ant literature is that the amount of earth excavated by one colony of leaf-cutter ants in Brazil weighed about forty-four tons—a construction job equivalent to the building of the Great Wall of China.

The Benefits of Ants

This book is intended to show you how to outwit ants that invade your personal space in numbers you cannot tolerate (which is different for everyone) or that threaten your home's physical structure or environment. It is not intended as a pro-ant diatribe or even a general dialogue on how you should learn to love ants or talk to the animals. That said, I cannot help but remind readers that ants are not just pests—in fact, they are only pests when humans come into the picture. They serve important roles in the environment, the ecology, and the very essence of our planet. And they can even help us.

For instance, ants prey on other insects that are considered pests by humans, including ticks, grubs, pillbugs, black cutworms, and many caterpillars. Their value as predators of termites is noted in the guide *Common-Sense Pest Control*: "Many ants are predators of termites. When ants gain access to termite nests, they are capable of destroying the entire colony."[8]

Ants also do the important work of cleaning up dead plants and animals and other debris, which they scavenge for the protein many ant species need and like. They also improve the soil by aerating it and adding organic matter, much in the manner of earthworms.

The message? Don't be too quick to eradicate every ant within ten square acres of your home. Take the preventive measures outlined in the following chapters seriously. Keep ants from becoming pests, and you won't have to eradicate them. And if they do make themselves a little more at home in and around your house than you are comfortable with, take steps to control them in proportion to the size of the problem. After reading this book and understanding more about ants, you will not only learn how to outwit them, you will also end up appreciating them.

A Web site for ant lovers is www.antcolony.org, which was founded in 1998 by an international nonprofit association for people interested in ant colonies. Anyone interested in ant colony development can become a member. The site is intended to support hobbyists as well as educate the public on ants' positive qualities and provide information on how to live with and without them. You can watch ants close-up and in action on their video programs, as well as find out interesting facts about ants, look at amazing photomicrographs, get reading suggestions, and instructions for taking care of an ant colony.

Species: The Few That Torment Us and Some That Don't

J ust fewer than 10,000 species of ants have been identified around the world. It is generally estimated that another 5,000 to 10,000 more species exist that have not yet been identified. Of the identified number, a paltry 700 or so live in the U.S. and Canada. Of those 700, a mere twenty-five species pester humans, infiltrating our homes in a nonstop search for food, water, and shelter. Cuba alone has dozens of ants species, almost none of which are found anywhere else in the world.

Ants are so successful, other species even mimic them, including spiders of the genera *Micaria* and *Castianeira*. These mimics can make ant identification confusing. For example, the velvety tree ant is the common picnic pest we all love to hate, but the so-called velvet ant is actually an impersonator: They are really wasps that look like ants in winter coats.

There are very few species that humans need to concern themselves with as we go about our daily business; however, those few are not to be ignored. They can take over your house like distant relatives at the holidays, making themselves comfortable before you even realize what is going on. Some ants don't ever make it to a building, but prefer to pester out of doors. They settle exactly where you want to spread your blanket for a fun family picnic—only you were intending the fun family picnic to include just your own family, not a colony of 10,000 fire ants.

Don't despair. Just get to know the species of ants in your locale so that you can learn what it is you are trying to prevent. And if you are going on a vacation, say a camping trip in the South, check ahead of time about the local ants *before* you scuff that little lump of soil down and pitch your tent right over a teeming, and now angry, mound of ants. You may be able to appease them with a few gooey s'mores, but wouldn't you rather not have to?

The Pests

Pest ants, as they are commonly called when they interfere with humans, are composed of two groups: wall-nesting and ground-nesting. According to the *NPCA Field Guide to Structural Pests,* ten of those twenty-five species divide up as follows:

- **Wall-nesting:**
  - Carpenter ants
  - Crazy ants
  - Odorous house ants
  - Pharaoh ants
  - Thief ants
- **Ground-nesting:**
  - Argentine ants
  - Pavement ants
  - Little black ants
  - Velvety tree ants
  - Fire ants

The Most Common Ant Pests in the United States

In setting up your defense and attack strategy, it will be important to know something about these common pest ants. Here are some key facts on each to help you recognize them and understand what you are dealing with. We'll take them alphabetically.

Argentine Ants

The scientific name of the Argentine ant is *Linepithema humile.* They range in color from light brown to dark brown and in size from around ⅟₁₆ inch to ¼ inch long. They are said to have arrived in North America during the late 1800s aboard a ship bound for New Orleans, where they were first reported, and "quickly became public Pest number one." Joshua Tompkins captured the havoc these ants wrought: "The local cut-flower industry withered, and Louisiana sugar farmers fought to save their crops. Entomologists nervously noted the intruders' tendency to wipe out native ants and other insects." All was not gloom and doom, though. "Residents of the poorer sections of town were grateful when their bedbugs suddenly vanished, and park visitors relished the disappearance of chiggers, but this didn't earn the arrivistes any points."[9]

Southern California, in particular, is plagued today with Argentine ants. Other areas of the U.S. one might also find them are the warmer southern states, but there have been isolated infestations reported farther north in Illinois, Maryland, Missouri, Oregon, and Washington.

The typical colony is relatively small, from several hundred to several thousand workers and dozens of queens. Since Argentine ants are rarely aggressive toward each other, small colonies will often merge, creating rather large colonies. The average maturity from egg to adult is seventy-four days—with dozens of queens per colony laying as many as sixty eggs per day, populations can get out of hand pretty quickly.

The Argentine ant thrives in a moist environment located close to a food source. They prefer to dine on sweets, such as sugar and syrup, but ultimately are not picky and will feed on anything available—meat, eggs, oil, you name it.

These ants prefer to stay out of doors but will go inside when the weather becomes too dry or too wet, or when they can't find any food and must explore inside to expand their search. They'll crawl over anything and everything, carrying any disease-causing organisms they pick up along the way, happy to track them into your house, over your kitchen counters, or wherever else they make themselves at home.

Carpenter Ants

The carpenter ant most common in the eastern U.S. goes by the scientific name *Camponotus pennsylvanicus*, while *C. moduc* is the species common in the West. Whatever you call them, they can be found across the entire country and are the ants most often referred to when we talk of household pests. They are large as ants go, reaching as much as ½ inch, with queens a little larger.

Since carpenter ants have no stinger, they can't sting; but their well-developed mandibles can deliver quite a bite, further inflamed with an injection of formic acid.

Carpenter ant colonies, as large as 15,000 workers strong, usually seek out already compromised wood for their nesting sites, especially moist wood. Not only do they need a constant supply of moisture, but moisture problems also make wood softer and therefore easier to work with. Many human habitats are great sources of wood, and they will enter around windows and doors, utility lines, or on plants that come in contact with a building. Once they've gotten a nest well under way, they'll be content to chomp on any uncompromised wood as the nest expands. Outside, carpenter ants will nest in rotting logs, wood fence posts, old firewood, and dead parts of live trees.

Their preferred food sources are almost anything—sweets, oils, eggs, or meat. They will even feed on insects and other arthropods. And they will happily destroy your house's structural integrity when they set up housekeeping to take advantage of the warmth, moisture, and proximity to their favorite foods it offers. In order to severely effect your house's structure, however, the colony will need to have been hard at work for several years, so constant vigilance pays off.

Crazy Ants

Paratrechina longicornis acquired its common name from its workers' habit of running around haphazardly in search of food. The crazy ant inhabits the entire U.S. but in the northern climates it will only be found indoors since the species cannot withstand cold temperatures.

Crazy ants are tiny, only ⅟₁₆ inch to ⅛ inch long, and their antennae and legs are long in proportion to their small bodies. According to the NPCA (National Pest Control Association), these ants haven't been the subject of the same intense studies that some other ant species have, but some basics are known. Their colonies average around 2,000 workers and somewhere between eight and forty queens. They have been observed abandoning nests and moving to new ones; their outdoor nests tend to be pretty close to the surface. Crazy ants, like most ants, eat any food, but they prefer sweets and insects.

Fire Ants

The legendary fire ant comes in several species in the U.S., including *Solenopsis xyloni*, which is the southern fire ant found from California to southern South Carolina and northern Florida; *S. invicta*, the red imported fire ant found in the southeastern U.S. and Virginia through Texas; and the black imported fire ant *S. richteri*, which is somewhat limited in range to Mississippi and Alabama; finally, *S. geminata*, known as the "tropical fire ant" is found in the moist tropical regions of the southeastern U.S.

Fire ants, since their importation to the U.S. in the late 1920s or early 1930s, have infested more than nine southern states and over 275 million acres. In Texas alone, annual estimates of crop damage caused by fire ants range in the millions of dollars.[10]

The different species of fire ants are distinguished by the size of their antenna and mouthparts. Their nests also differ; for instance, the red imported fire ant creates mounds above the ground that raise up an inch and a half or so, while the mounds of the southern fire ant are flat and wider, covering two to four square feet. Both have long stingers sticking out of their bodies that inflict painful stings.

The red imported fire ant averages many thousands per colony, from 80,000 to 250,000. The queens produce around 1,500 eggs per day that develop from egg to ant in approximately a month. Workers' lifespans are a couple months, while queens live approximately two to six years.

According to the Web site, www.antcolony.org ("the definitive source for ant enthusiasts"), fire ants are comfortable in both urban and rural settings, bothering everything from humans to animals and crops. Fire ants typically nest in the ground, but they will enter buildings where food is available. They also have been found nesting in electrical junction boxes, including those that control traffic lights. The NPCA warns that if the nest gets too large they can even cause electrical malfunctions.

Fire ants feed on plants and animals and look for food everywhere. Research at Colorado State University shows that in a relentless search for sustenance, "they damage crops such as soybeans, eggplant, corn, okra, strawberries, and potatoes by feeding directly on the plants or by protecting other insects that damage the crops. They chew the bark and growing tips of citrus trees and feed on the fruit." And they destroy property as well as crops when their "mounds interfere with farming and mowing operations and turn recreational fields into disfigured moonscapes. Fire ants have caused sections of roads to collapse by removing soil from under the asphalt."[11] Fire ants have proven themselves especially a nuisance in the national parks system, rendering campsite areas unusable.

Their sting is not known to be life threatening in general, but they can cause serious medical problems in certain circumstances. They do have some redeeming value, feeding on significant pests such as boll weevils, sugarcane borers, ticks, and cockroaches.

Leaf-Cutter Ants

There are as many as fifteen species of leaf-cutter ants (genus *Atta*) found in the southern U.S. in Louisiana and Texas. These little farmers grow their own food in a very interesting way by accumulating vegetation in their nests. They cut off pieces of leaves, carrying them over their heads to their nest, which gives them the nickname of "parasol ants."

They don't, however, eat the leaves. Instead, they mash them into a paste that serves as host to a fungus, which the ants then eat. This fungus is thought to be almost exclusive to leaf-cutter ant colonies and is rarely found in the wild. In *Journey to the Ants*, Bert Hölldobler and Edward O. Wilson highlight the voracious appetite of the leaf-cutter ant for this fungus, pointing out that "each colony can daily consume as much vegetation as a grown cow."[12] Although not considered household pests, leaf cutters destroy billions of dollars in Central and South American crops annually. Ironically, they also serve an important purpose, similar to the more likeable earthworm, in aerating the soil to make it more hospitable for planting.

The leaf-cutter queen can produce as many as 150 million daughters in her reproductive lifetime with just a few of these becoming queens themselves. The size of mature leaf-cutter colonies can reach into the millions.

In the Disney movie *A Bug's Life*, an ant inventor teams up with a group of other insects to keep a gang of grasshoppers from terrorizing his colony. This fun animated film has lots of beneath-the-surface references that only the ant enthusiast would catch—for instance, the future queen of the colony is Princess Atta, *Atta* being the genus of the leaf-cutter ant. There are many other aspects that aren't ant-perfect, though. For instance, the queen would never have taken Flick, the film's star, as her sole mate.

Little Black Ants

Monomorium minimum may be small in size (averaging ⅟₁₆ inch with an insignificant stinger), but they make their way everywhere in the U.S. Although prevalent, they have not been heavily studied. Like most ants, their colonies contain many queens. They locate their nests in decaying wood or compromised masonry, and can be found in the yard under rocks, fallen logs, or in open areas. They are among the species that are partial to the honeydew collected from aphids (see more on this behavior in Chapter Three), so any plants that are attacked by aphids will also attract the little black ant. The colonies found in buildings—rarely teeming with plant life—are usually satellite colonies of a main colony that can be found somewhere nearby.

Odorous House Ants

The *NPCA Field Guide to Structural Pests* describes most ants as having at least some faint odor when crushed. For the odorous house ant (*Tapinoma sessile*), though, the odor—described as "pungent, rotten-coconut-like"—is matched to its name. These smelly little buggers are found throughout the U.S.

Colonies of odorous house ants are moderate in size, ranging from several hundred to around 10,000, with several queens that produce four to five generations per year. Workers and queens live for several years and colonies do not exhibit hostility toward others.

They prefer sweets and are found in kitchens around sinks and cupboards and tend to nest in warm places within the walls, such as near your hot water pipes. They have a habit of lifting their lower bodies and running around frantically when disturbed.

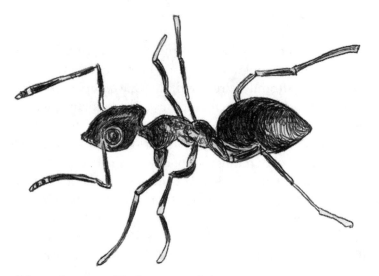

Odorous house ant (Tapinoma sessile)

Pavement Ant

As might be assumed from its common name, *Tetramorium cae-spitum* lives around cracks in pavement. Pavement ants are mostly found in the eastern U.S., California, and Washington. They've been here a while—it's assumed they came to the U.S. from Europe with the early colonists.

Pavement ants live in relatively large colonies. Although they are primarily outdoor ants—the kind you would expect to find in ground-level masonry walls and foundations—they will venture farther inside to nest in insulation and under floors. They also bite and sting, but not aggressively. A real meat-and-potatoes sort, the pavement ant is a grease- and protein-lover, and is drawn to food sources of these types.

Pharaoh Ants

Pharaoh ants (*Monomorium pharaonis*) are native to the African region around Egypt. They received their common name based on the belief that they were one of the plagues of Egypt. It's thought that during the era of the Pharaohs, they were responsible for spreading disease.

Although there are no ancient pyramids in sight, pharaoh ants are found throughout the U.S. Their colonies are huge, sometimes teeming with hundreds of thousands of workers and several hundred reproducing females. Workers are short-lived, dying after only a few weeks. Queens live less than a year, and males die within a couple of weeks after mating.

Pharaoh ants tend to nest indoors near food, water, and warmth, but are also found in debris on flat roofs and in gutters. They are common problems in places where commercial food handling is prevalent. They have been known to live outside year round in the extreme southern climates, but they cannot survive in cold temperatures.

Thief Ants

The thief ant (*Solenopsis molesta*), one of the smallest of the pest ants, earns its name from its survival tactics—establishing itself near other ants' nests, then stealing their food and young. The thief ant is golden in color, native to the U.S., and found throughout the country. Its stinger is small and therefore not very effective.

The thief ant and the pharaoh ant are often mistaken for each other, but if you are prone to walking around with a magnifying glass in your pocket, you can easily distinguish the two, since the thief ant's antennae have ten segments, and the pharaoh ant's have twelve. If you get real close, you'll also notice that a thief ant's club has two segments, opposed to a pharaoh ant's three.

Thief ant colonies are moderately sized, numbering anywhere from a few hundred to several thousand with several queens. They will often feed on dead rodents, which is why they are assumed to carry disease. Also, they will often head inside during hot weather where they will feed on almost anything, although the thief ant's preference is high-protein food.

Outside, thief ants will nest almost anywhere, from out in the open to under objects or in hidden cavities.

Velvety Tree Ants

Although there are many species of the velvety tree ant, *Liometopum occidentale* is the main culprit. According to The *NPCA Field Guide to Structural Pests*, these ants are found in Oregon, Wyoming, Utah, Nevada, California, Colorado, Arizona, New Mexico, and Texas. They get their common name from their velvety black abdomen.

The velvety tree ant colony is usually large, with a single queen. Colonies are found in trees, in stumps, and under stones, especially along streams. They are common to cottonwood and oak trees. When crushed (a favorite identifying technique of the NPCA manual), they give off a strong odor, similar to the odorous house ant.

These are the ants that are major picnic pests. A trail of hundreds will tramp into houses and homes, usually in search of sweets. They are active mainly in the morning and at night, and if the colony is disturbed, they may swarm and bite.

Less Common but Interesting Ants

> "Often as I watched the marauder ants' tightly orchestrated activities, the thousands of individuals seemed to merge into a single dynamic pattern. It was as if all the ants had united to form one great living creature."
> —Mark W. Moffett, *National Geographic*, August 1996

Some of these ants are common to the U.S., but aren't considered pests in general. Others will only plague you in faraway lands. A few interesting facts about some of the more exotic ants may make you feel a little better about the level of pestilence you may need to deal with!

Acrobat Ant *(Crematogaster)*

These little guys, found all over the country, earn this moniker from their habit of raising the abdomen over the head and thorax, a feat they perform when particularly disturbed. They like Styrofoam insulation and have even been known to nest in the insulation around electrical wires, making them potentially dangerous. They will also enter around the dampened areas of a structure.

Army Ants (*Eciton*)

There are twelve known species of the Army ant genus *Eciton*. Miniature army ants (*E. neivamyrmex*) are found in the western and southern U.S. They mostly stay underground and have not been the subject of extensive study. They are, as might be expected, tiny in size, have phases of intense movement alternated with stationary periods, and prey on other species.

Basiceros Ant *(Basiceros)*

These ants are found in the forests of Central and South America. They have many behavioral characteristics that are unusual in the ant world. For instance, when their nest is disturbed, instead of reeling in mass hysteria as most ants do, Basiceros ants freeze in place for as long as several minutes. And unlike other species, these odd fellows spend almost no time grooming each other or themselves. Instead, according to Hölldobler and Wilson, they use their scruffy exterior as a version of camouflage.

Bulldog Ants (*Myrmecia gulosa*)

These Australian ants have a vicious sting and bite, and the ability to kill even a human when attacking in sufficient numbers. They are among the few species that produce some of their own food, laying certain eggs to become future generations and using others as a source of nutrition.

Giant Hunting Ants (*Dinoponera grandis*)

This is the largest known ant in the world, and it is found deep in the Amazon jungles. A direct result of their large size is a pair of massive mandibles.

Ghost Ants (*Tapinoma melanocephalum*)

As might be expected, the ghost ant is very pale in color. It is found mostly in warmer climates in the south and Hawaii. They nest in many places in the house, including wall cavities, behind baseboards, and in any other out-of-the-way spot. Outside, however, they will nest in dirt and tree cavities, and will take up residence in potted plants.

Harvester Ants (*Pogonomyrmex barbartus*)

Rather large in size, harvester ants create huge mounds that can be found in the southwestern U.S., and that measure from twenty to thirty feet across and as much as six feet deep. Their preferred food is seeds, and they are known to move seeds outside the nest on sunny days to dry them out. They can also sting viciously, but the stinger is blunt and can only penetrate tender skin, making children more vulnerable than adults. People who keep horned lizards as pets are familiar with harvester ants, which are a favorite lizard food.

Honey Ants (*Myrmecocystus melliger*)

The honey ant is unique for the extremely large gaster it uses to store the honeydew and nectar it spends most of its time collecting. Once it gets back to the nest it regurgitates its bounty to its sisters and the larvae in the nest. Some of them simply function as literal honey pots—they hang from the ceiling with their distended gasters and provide a nectar-filling station for other members of the colony. Honey ants are found in the southwestern U.S. and Mexico and have long been considered a delicacy by some Native American peoples.

Marauder Ants (*Pheidologeton diversus*)

These tropical ants make substantial and complex trails while searching for food. Workers constantly tend the main trails and the smaller offshoots extending out from them. Thousands of ants use these trails. Although in general they do not bite and have no stinger, marauder ants are known to restrain prey, tear off limbs, and move the helpless but still-alive prey to their nests.

Singaporean Antler-Jawed Ants

The mandibles of these ants open 280 degrees and have two trigger hairs that cause the lethal jaws to spring open when they touch prey.

South American Ant

This rare ant has its head tucked into a crab-like shell for protection from its enemies.

Trap-jaw Ant (*Odontomachus*)

This is a tropical species that is found only in the Deep South. They have powerful mandibles recorded to bite at proportionately faster speeds than a bullet from a rifle—in fact, their mandibles are the "fastest of any anatomical structure ever recorded in the animal kingdom!"[13] They quickly follow up their ferocious bite with a sting when threatened.

Keep an Ant List

Birdwatchers are notorious for keeping life lists of all the bird species they've managed to spot throughout the years. Maybe learning a little about the many fascinating species of ants will entice you to keep an ant life list, recording all the species you've located and even a few notes on their behavior! You will never be able to hang a clock in your living room that imitates the sounds of different ants the way you can for birds, but an "Annual Ant Count" may be in your future.

The company Insect Lore sells educational products on insects of many kinds, including ants. Fun products include plastic ants, Uncle Milton ant farms, and educational charts showing ant anatomy and life cycles. Insect Lore can be reached at 1–800-LIVE-BUG.

3

Anatomy and Behavior

"Ants live long enough to learn from experience."
—Peter Farb, *The Insects*

You won't find an ant sitting around watching the tube in the evening, wishing there was something more interesting to do. No one has to beg an ant to take out the trash. They are busy creatures—the adults play round-the-clock nursemaids to the young, a constant stream of workers head to and from the grocery store (once they locate one), and they are foraging, hunting, transporting, and ensuring the proper storage of food almost nonstop.

In fact, one of the most interesting things about an ant colony is that it functions at a high rate of effectiveness, even though there is no controlling figure telling each ant what to do. The queen is the central figure of the colony, but she does not hand out daily orders or direct each ant to a specific task. Ants just instinctively go about the colony's business. Research shows, however, that these instincts are actually guided by a chemical transformation between the queen and the workers, and between one ant and another—a common colonial odor keeps the ants on track in their common goal of keeping the colony thriving.

Being aware of ant behavior, and the differences among the species, is the key to preventing and controlling pest ants in your home. In order to take successful measures to keep them out of your living space, it is necessary to know their nesting habits, food preferences, and when, why, and how they may choose to enter a house.

Before we get into the well-studied topic of ant behavior, some simple anatomy lessons need to come first.

Ant Anatomy

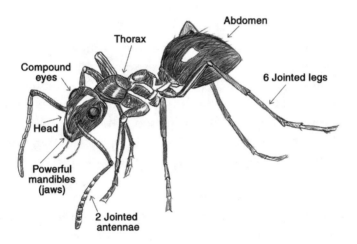

Scientific Classification

The basic scientific classification of ants is:

Kingdom: Anamalia
Phyllum: Arthropoda
Class: Insecta
Order: Hymenoptera

Ant Specs

Ants are insects. They are found everywhere on Earth except the Arctic and Antarctica. All insects share the physical traits of having three body parts—the head, thorax, and abdomen—jointed legs, a pair of antennae, and an exoskeleton.

All members of the order Hymenoptera have bodies that show a distinct waist, making bees, wasps, and a select few other insects close relatives of the ant. Nothing in nature is without reason. The waist of an ant comes in one or two moving parts, adding to its maneuverability in the tight, twisting quarters of an ant colony.

Although ants' average size range is from .08 inches to 1.2 inches there are itty-bitty ants too. Harvard professor Edward O. Wilson—recognized as the dean of biodiversity studies—gives an example of the enormous size disparity within the insect order: "A colony of the world's smallest ant could dwell comfortably inside the braincase of the world's largest ant." [14]

Ants have six jointed legs, all attached at the thorax. They have compound eyes with up to 1,000 lenses in each eye, and each lens is attached to its own nerve ending. The eye does not move as a unit; each individual lens takes in its segment of the surroundings, giving the ant a highly grainy view of its landscape. The more lenses, the less grainy the picture is.

A nerve cord, much like our spinal cord, runs from the brain through the length of the ant's body. The heart is located in the abdomen segment, as is the stomach, the crop, and the rectum.

Non-worker males and queens have wings until after they mate. After the nuptial flight, the queen no longer needs her wings—in fact, they would be too cumbersome when she holes up in her confined chamber deep within the nest for the rest of her life—so she loses them, often removing them herself. The winged males, however, die shortly after mating with the queen. The relatively quick disappearance of winged ants is probably why we don't think of ants as flying insects, even though at some stage many are capable of flight.

The winged members of the ant colony, however, create some confusion when determining whether you have an ant or a termite infestation. If the insects you find in your house have wings, look closely at them. A main distinguishing characteristic between ants and termites is that, although both have two sets of wings, an ant's second set is smaller in size than the first. And ants' wings have fewer veins running through them than do termites'. Further distinctions between these two home wreckers are outlined in Chapter Four.

To Sting or Not To Sting?

Some ants sting, some don't. Typically, the ones that don't have a stinger, don't sting. Yet others that do possess a stinger don't use it because it's dull and largely ineffective. It's like hunting with a gun but no bullets—why bother pulling it out if it doesn't work? The ants that do use their stingers as a means of defense or to kill their prey often have a very effective stinger indeed.

One rule of thumb when sizing up an insect opponent is that an ant with a two-node pedicel—the part between the thorax and the abdomen—tends to sting. This allows for a fuller range of motion, as the body, with its exterior suit of armor, is better able to articulate and direct the stinger.

Putting the Squeeze On

Besides having a potent sting, some ants pack a decent bite. Mandibles vary greatly from species to species, but the ants that chew wood or bite defensively have impressive sets of choppers. Interestingly, the mandibles and the sting are related. Ant researcher John H. Sudd explains this relationship: "In stinging, most ants seize the enemy and apply their sting close to the bite. . . . It is clear that the mandibles provide the purchase for thrusting in the sting."[15]

Mandibles are critical: They not only have a great deal to do with the type of food an ant species eats, but they also actually determine the structure of the entire head. Some mandibles are tapered long and thinly like a pair of tongs, and some are short and fat, meeting in a circle like the rings of a three-ring binder.

Without the mandibles, ants would be mostly incapable of engaging with the world. They use them to dig soil and excavate wood for nests, to delicately carry around eggs, to impale their prey, slice up lunch, and, of course, to ward off enemies in the throes of battle.

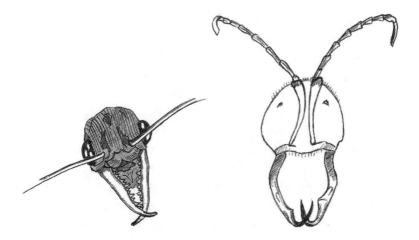

The incredible ant mandibles.

The Mind of an Ant

Each worker ant has a brain consisting of approximately a million nerve cells. The average human being, who is one million times as heavy as an ant, has a brain of approximately 100 billion nerve cells.[16]

Life Cycle

As a child did you ever collect a Monarch caterpillar from the underside of a milkweed leaf and watch it go through the phases that transformed it from an earthbound crawly thing to a delicate, fluttering butterfly? Well, during its short life, the ant goes through the same typical four stages—egg, larvae, pupae, and adult—as any insect that metamorphoses from one form to something very different.

The Egg

Ant eggs are laid exclusively by queens. During her brief nuptial flight, before a queen settles into a life of egg-production in the nest, she is inseminated with all the sperm she will need throughout her lifetime. Later, as an egg leaves her body, it is either fertilized or passes through without insemination. The fertilized eggs develop into females, and the unfertilized eggs become males, a characteristic known as haplodiploidy.

As in large human child-care centers where infants are cared for separately from toddlers and older preschoolers, pre-adult ants are all kept in specific chambers of the nest according to developmental stage, and those chambers are further broken down by size. As the egg emerges from the queen, a worker promptly carries it off. She stores it in the appropriate chamber,

A queen carpenter ant.

which changes according to the size of the egg. All three pre-adult stages are moved around the nest by the workers to keep them at the perfect temperature. William Morton Wheeler noted this behavior in his 1913 work, *Ants: Their Structure, Development, and Behavior*: "[D]uring very warm weather, the young may be brought to the surface after nightfall. In the dry deserts of western Texas, I have even seen *Ischnomyrmex cockerelli* bring its larvae and pupae out onto the large crater of the nest about nine P.M., and carry them leisurely to and fro, much as human nurses wheel their charges about the city parks in the cool of the evening."[17]

The Larvae

A grub-like larva emerges from the egg with a head and distinct sections. It's handled with care and fed by the adult workers, while significant internal and external changes are going on. At the end of the larval stage, some ants spin a cocoon in preparation for the pupal stage.

The Pupae

Whether under cover of a cocoon or not, the ant uses the pupal stage to make its final transformation into adulthood. The new adults often need help being freed from the pupa skin, a task performed by their attentive nursemaids.

The Adult

After all it takes for an ant to come into the world in the form we most recognize, the adults that become female workers often live as little as a few weeks, though some live as long as seven years. Unfortunately, for the males, death comes right after mating with a queen. And the pampered queens, defying the human notion that a life span is extended with exercise and fresh air, live out their lives basically immobile. They are fed, groomed, and completely tended to by the workers, and do

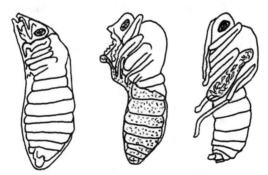

The emerging pupa.

nothing but produce eggs—yet some of them have been recorded to live as long as fifteen years.

Behavior

As simple as an ant's anatomy is, its behavior is incredibly complex. Entire books have been written on the subject, and some scientists have spent whole careers studying the inner workings of the ant colony, often covering just a single species. And although different species have significant differences in their colonial setups, ant colonies in general exhibit many similarities.

The Colony and the Concept of the Superorganism

The most compelling trait of ants is the natural inclination to act as a "superorganism"—one individual is insignificant, but when it acts in conjunction with every other ant in the colony, the superorganism of a colony acting as one is substantial indeed and operates as a well-oiled, finely tuned machine. The need for these social insects to live in a colony is of supreme importance to ant success.

Each individual knows his or her job within the system and seems to have no desire to stray from that job. In fact, any individual is willing and often does sacrifice its existence for the sake of the colony. With such devoted individuals, the superorganism remains well-equipped, though it seems to exist for no greater reason than to constantly restock its supply of microorganisms—the individual ants themselves—keeping the colony at the optimum size for its well-being, and ensuring the good of all the individuals.

This superorganism mentality makes sense in a creature so small it seems almost inconsequential. But the naturalist Charles

Darwin had a problem with this point of view, in light of his own research and theory about all species' inclination toward natural selection and survival of the fittest. If any species is to survive over the long haul, his reasoning goes, the individuals with the characteristics most fitting to survival would be the ones to perpetuate the species.

In the superorganism, however, the only member of supreme importance is the queen. And she is a super-producer, mating with a troop of males who die shortly thereafter. This stands in contrast to Darwin's reasoning. In fact, nothing about ant reproduction seems to fit Darwin's theory. Or does it?

The Caste System

Although looked upon with disdain by human societies of the free world, ant colonies are mapped out in a caste system composed of three distinct castes:

Queens: Females who are capable of reproduction may attempt to become a queen. Some ant colonies support dozens, perhaps even hundreds, of queens. But becoming a queen of your own ant colony is fraught with peril and begins as a lonely undertaking. This is where Darwin's theory pops up again in the ant world, where only the fittest queens survive to found their own colonies. When they do, the queens begin their lives serving as egg-laying machines, upon whom the entire colony revolves, from attending to her and attending to her eggs.

A fertile female who desires to become queen of her own colony makes an arduous pilgrimage to a new site. "Only the very best endowed individuals live to preserve the species from extinction," explains William Morton Wheeler. To him, there is "no better example of survival of the fittest through natural selection" than these pilgrim ants. "The vast majority after starting their shal-

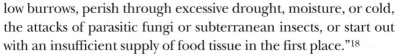

low burrows, perish through excessive drought, moisture, or cold, the attacks of parasitic fungi or subterranean insects, or start out with an insufficient supply of food tissue in the first place."[18]

Winged males: These are the fertile adults who mate with the queen during her nuptial flight. Although obviously of great importance to the creation of a colony, this act represents the fulfillment of their lives and they die soon after mating.

Workers: These adults are the sterile females who perform the hard work of keeping the entire nest thriving, including nursing, housekeeping, hunting, and soldiering.

The Daily Grind

Not only do ants have a system that predestines a particular sex to a specific job, but the worker ant population also has a caste-like system, which directs the specialized type of work each ant performs. Some ants attend to the queen: They feed her, groom her, and collect her eggs as they leave her body. Other ants are nursemaids, attending every need of the young at every stage of development. Still others take care of the pantry, hunting for and collecting food for the colony. Within these categories is still further specialization, with some ants attending to the eggs, some to the larvae, and some having very specific foraging activities, often depending on the species of ant. There is some indication that the size of the ant helps determine its specialty.

Communication

Although clearly paling in comparison to the super-connected world of humans, ants have a fairly sophisticated ability to communicate with each other. And communication among individuals is important to the overall well-being of the colony.

One of the main methods of communication is touch. The antennae have as many as thirteen joints and provide one key way for pest control experts to firmly identify a species. Ants put these highly articulated appendages to good use by passing information to one another. They spend a lot of time cleaning these sensitive devices, allowing them to detect flavors, sounds, and odors among colony members.

Ants communicate via taste and smell also, producing special chemicals that provide information for other ants to read. This ant eau-de-cologne creates a signature smell that allows members of the colony to recognize each other. If a strange ant wanders into the colony, it will be immediately recognized as an outsider and will most likely be expelled or even killed.

The other vital function that these chemicals and smells serve is to make a scent trail, known as a pheromone trail, to and from food sources to the nest. Ants are a touchy-feely bunch, with the express purpose of passing the odor of the nest among their colony mates.

Early research in the area suggests that ants also have sensory ability in their feet, through two tiny hairs called sensilla. Researchers have tentatively concluded that these hairs may help the ants know they are on the right trail.

Cleanliness Is Next to Antliness?

Cleanliness is of supreme importance to most ant species, not only of the nest but also of themselves—especially their antennae.

Cleaning habits are different for different species, though. Some ants are reported to clean antennae with the strigil on the leg of the same side. Studies show that *Formica fusca* cleans one antenna with the leg on the same side while the other leg is being cleaned with the mouthparts.[19]

Food

Animals naturally crave what they need and hunt it down. If this can be said about grazing livestock, why not an ant? When horses lack a particular nutrient, they seek it out by choosing forage high in that specific nutrient or they'll find natural salt licks in the wild, which provide certain essential minerals. (It's interesting that "less intelligent" species instinctively know what to eat to stay alive while the super-intelligent human species requires dietary food pyramids and nutrition experts just to remind us we can't live on potato chips and soda alone!)

The worker ant assigned the task of hunting, foraging, or scouting for food spends all its waking hours in that pursuit (ants take little snoozes during the course of a day, and they even stretch and yawn when they wake up!). In some species, an ant that has found food can direct its nest mates there too.

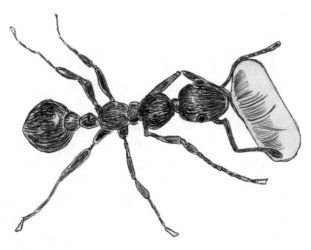

A fire ant.

Some species send out a "scout" who may attempt to bring food back to the nest by itself. If it can't, it returns to the nest—either empty-handed or with a manageable portion—and recruits other workers to return to the food source, following the scent trail it left on its way back to the nest.

According to a Colorado State University bulletin on fire ant control, the oldest and most expendable members of the fire ant colony head out from the nest to track down food sources, having a range of less than 100 feet from the nest. Any liquid food they run across they swallow, returning to the nest to re-gurgitate it to other members of the colony who don't have hunting and gathering duties.

Foraging activity can carry some of the most useful behav-ioral information to pest control experts. How an ant collects food and, of course, what it eats, is key in setting baits and poi-sons that will stop an ant colony in its tracks. Since, for example, the fire ant feeds other members of the colony, your extermina-tor knows that liquid baits will be eaten by the foragers and fed to friends and family.

Teaming Up

For ants, strength truly does come in numbers. But they also do numerous things in pairs or small groups. They are often grooming and licking each other, and a select group of workers constantly grooms the queen. They also exchange food from one ant's crop to another's.

In larger groups, they team up to move food or nest materi-als. Sometimes they even come together in order to move them-selves—connecting their bodies in large masses, intricately weaving their legs and antennae together to make a bridge for other ants to cross from one place to another.

Edward O. Wilson, in his essay "Ants and Cooperation," from *In Searh of Nature* discusses the giant tropical stinging ant's teamwork when bringing vital water to its nest mates:

> . . . a giant black worker ant . . . leaves her earthen nest and climbs a nearby shrub to a glistening cluster of dew. . . . Opening her mandibles, she collects a droplet of dew, and then returns to the nest. After pausing at the entrance to allow another worker to drink some of the water, she descends through vertical galleries until she reaches the brood chambers where the colony's immature young are kept. There she daubs part of her burden onto a cocoon and passes the rest to a thirsty larva.[20]

Farming

Some ant species have developed the sophisticated ability of growing their own food. Although they don't get out their little hoes and dig rows in the dirt and plant seeds, it is nonetheless an amazing process for ants that require a specific foodstuff for survival.

One such food is the fungus grown by the leaf-cutter ant. The workers spend a lot of time collecting—denuding trees, stealing their leaves, and cutting them up into sizes manageable enough to carry back to the nest. Once in the nest, however, they don't actually eat the leaves. Instead they gum them into a leaf-mash that proves to be fertile ground for the fungus that leaf cutters thrive on—a fungus known to grow almost exclusively in leaf-cutter nests, rather than in the wild. Most fungus-growing studies have focused on the famous leaf-cutter ants, other species are also known to grow their own food in a similar manner.

And ants are not only good fungus farmers, they're also excellent weeders. Researcher Cameron Currie of the University of Texas, Austin, reported that, when he put a piece of invasive fungus in a fungus garden of a leaf-cutter colony, he "thought this was going to be exciting. . . . But in about ten seconds, along comes an ant and picks it up and carries it to the dump, and it's all over."[21] Unlike me, whose garden quickly becomes a mass of plants so tangled it's difficult to distinguish the weeds from the edibles, ants are attentive gardeners.

Harvester ants are big on seeds as foodstuffs. Although they don't do much in the way of actual farming, some of their harvesting practices manipulate their caches of seeds to their advantage. For instance, to discourage mold and, therefore, spoilage, the workers will carry the seeds out of the nest to dry in the sun for the day, then carry them back to the nest's storage areas—easy for you and me, but a lot of work for an ant! They

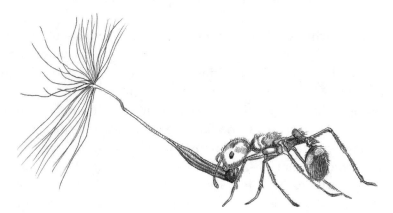

A harvester ant.

will also bite off the sprout end of the seed to prevent it from sprouting after it's been carried into the confines of the nest.

There are even ants who tend other insects as if they were livestock, milking them for their juices. The insects they husband include aphids, mealy-bugs, and scale insects, which all produce so-called "honeydew," a secretion the ants milk them for. Ants tap an aphid's abdomen with an antenna to elicit the honeydew secretion. And since aphids consume more fluid than they need themselves, they often have an overflow seeping out of their bodies. The ants will provide a level of protection to the aphids from other insects, which allows them to thrive on your favorite plant. They even go so far as to gather the aphids and their eggs before winter, providing them a safe, warm haven in the ant nest.

Defense

Members of an ant colony rally to the defense of the colony and its queens if invaded by an offending party. It doesn't even have to be a living intruder. William Morton Wheeler noticed during his research that "in the presence of some substance that they cannot remove, such as a strong-smelling liquid," nearly all ants will react similarly. "They throw pellets of earth or any other debris on the substance, sometimes in sufficient amount to bury it completely."[22]

Intruders of their own kind, however, are significant sources of ant angst. Ants and humans have something sad and significant in common: they are a danger to their own species. Swiss myrmecologist Augustus Forel writes: "The ant's most dangerous enemies are other ants, just as man's most dangerous enemies are other men." [23] Another ant researcher, John H. Sudd notes that "ants do not usually tolerate intruders into their nests. They usually attack them and often kill them, overpowering them by large numbers called up by alarm scents or other signals. Even members of other colonies of the same species are attacked."[24]

Symbiotic Relationships

The dairy farmer relationship between the ant and the aphid is well documented, as is the relationship between ants and the caterpillar of Lycaenid butterflies. Again, like the aphid, the ant induces the caterpillar to produce a liquid that the ant consumes straight from the source. The ants milk their caterpillar-cows either "in the field" or back at the ranch. The return favor is, as might be expected, protection for the caterpillar from enemies.

One other example of insect symbiosis is the ant and the mealy bug. The mealy bugs are carried to their feeding sites by several species of rainforest ants. Once there, worker ants attend to the mealy bugs and continually harvest their honeydew as they feed.[25]

Not only do ants enjoy symbiotic relationships with other creatures but with plants as well. In the tropics, for instance, stinging ants take up housekeeping in the thorn of the acacia tree after hollowing the thorn out to accommodate themselves. The tree provides a syrupy sustenance while the ants protect the tree from other species of insects that might prove harmful.[26]

The well-known fungus growing practice of the *Atta*, or leaf-cutter species, is perhaps one of the most pure symbiotic relationships. The ant lives only on the fungus that grows on the leaf mash, and that type of fungus grows almost exclusively in leaf-cutter colonies.

Strange and Amazing Behaviors

Ants may be small, but they are not lacking in eccentricities. Here are a few oddities that might make good cocktail party banter:

- The Argentine ant is known to conduct "regicide"—it will murder the reigning queen and make way for a new regime.
- The carnivorous army ants found in tropical America (mostly Louisiana in North America) have no permanent home but make one out of their own bodies. As many as 150,000 ants will cluster together hanging from a branch or in the hollow of a tree, with the queen and young protected inside.
- In making its nest of leaves, the weaver ant uses larvae from the colony to sew together the leaves. The larvae produces silk, which the adult weaver stimulates into production as it carries the larvae along the leaves stitching them together.
- Slave-making species of ants exist whose livelihood is to raid other species' nests and steal their young, which are either allowed to hatch out back in their own nests to be used as slaves or as food. Some raids even involve the queens, who kill the other queens and their daughters, then take over the orphaned brood that, once they reach adulthood, become slaves to the murderesses.
- Leaf cutters invite the smaller non-cutting workers to hitch rides on the leaves that are being carried back to the nest. These hitchhikers are thought to fend off phorid flies during the trip to the nest. The phorid flies will inject an egg into a leaf cutter that chews its way out through the

brain, killing the ant. So the leaf cutters' tiny hitchhiking brethren serve as lifesavers.[27]

- The pheromone trails ants are known to leave to guide them back, and to lead other ants to a food source, don't work as well outside where they are exposed to the elements. Ants are thought instead, according to research conducted at The Sussex Centre for Neuroscience in England, to memorize the visual landmarks along the path to their food.[28]

- *Science News* has reported that "ants can hear with their knees, picking up vibrations humming through leaves or nests or even the ground." They are thought to pick up communications this way registering any number of important things such as "lost relatives, great food, free rides for hitchhikers, caterpillars in search of ant partners, and impending doom."[29]

- The wood ant species *Formica polyctena* forms a high nest mound in the forest floor, a structural advantage that "increases the rate of warming in early spring, allowing the ants a head start over their competitors."[30]

These are just a few of the amazing stories of ant behavior. It just doesn't pay to underestimate the tiny ant!

Ants in the House

"The question I'm asked most often about ants is 'What do I do about the ones in my kitchen?' And my answer is always the same: 'Watch where you step.' Be careful of little lives. Feed them crumbs of coffeecake. They also like bits of tuna and whipped cream. Get a magnifying glass. Watch them closely. And you will be as close as any person may ever come to seeing social life as it might evolve on another planet."
—Edward O. Wilson, "In the Company of Ants"

The old saying goes that the only things that are certain in life are death and taxes, but "seeing an ant in your house" could safely be added to that list. Who hasn't seen an ant walk across the kitchen counter stumbling upon that one crumb you missed with the sponge?

Chances are you don't panic about one ant in your kitchen, maybe not even two. But when the ants start bringing in their cousins, nephews, great-nieces, and the rest of the clan, you will definitely want to take action. No matter how many ants you see, rest assured there are many, many more where they came from.

None seem so determined as the Argentine ant, found in many parts of the country but a real scourge in California. In Joshua Tompkins's "Empire of the Ants," homeowners' descriptions of this ant's enemy invasions are impressive: "They were coming out of the sockets, out of the tub," says one especially plagued woman. "They were coming out of my purse like a volcano." It's no wonder our imagined aliens often look remarkably like ants.

Ant problems in your house really mean ant problems outside. Ants don't really want to be in your house per se, they just go where food is convenient and the temperature suits their needs. For the most part, the offending colonies are set up outside your home, and the foraging workers happen to strike a path into your kitchen, find your food, and call in reinforcements.

A Three-Pronged Approach

The approach to keeping your home relatively ant-free is a three-pronged one. The first is to keep them out to begin with. While it's nearly impossible to eliminate every potential entry point, it is possible to reduce them to just a few, and to be diligent about checking for new potential entry points once or twice a year.

The second prong is to avoid making your home appealing to ants—in other words, once they wander in, don't encourage them to return with all their friends and family. Don't leave cookies and milk or the dirty butter knife from last night's midnight snack on the counter. Don't allow moisture to invade your wood for the ants' nest-building ease. There are dozens of things you can do and can avoid in order to make your home undesirable to an ant.

The last prong of the three-prong approach is chemical pest control. They got in; now you need to patch up the entry points and preferably eliminate the ants by killing the invading colony off or at least reducing the population. If you don't, you will immediately be host to ongoing ant parties.

I prefer to encourage concentrating on the first two prongs of the approach, and pest control experts prefer that too. Insecticides are poisons no matter what way you look at them, and the less we need to use them the better off the whole planet is. Nonetheless, there is a time when the benefit outweighs the cost—environmental or otherwise—and chemicals become necessary. And when they do, I recommend, as you will read about in more detail later in this chapter, that their use is best left to experts who have been trained in how to use as little as possible in the most effective and safest manner.

Prong One: Keep Out!

As mentioned earlier, the first prong in the three-pronged approach is to keep ants from invading your house in the first place. This is not quite as easy as it sounds. Even the biggest of ants are tiny. They can squeeze themselves through a slot narrower than the width of the page you are reading—the thought of how many places around the perimeter of your house that fit this description is mind boggling.

In order to deter ants, you will certainly need to do the best you can to seal your home from creatures that would just as soon take advantage of any warmth or nourishment you might be able to provide—after all, their survival over millions of years is not without reason. But you can caulk and seal until your arms fall off and you might never completely defend your castle against the relentless ant. And most homeowners will not go to these prophylactic extremes; it is human nature to wait until ants are spotted before attacking the issue of their potential entry points. By the time you notice any significant sign of ants in your house, your job is probably already a little tougher than it would have been.

That said, there are still plenty of things you can do to keep the invasion to a small band of foot soldiers instead of the whole army. After some tips on how to do that, we will move on to things that might make your abode less appealing to any ants that slip through your new and improved fortress.

Cracks and Crevices

If the tiniest of cracks can give entry to your home, a crack of significant width is a wide-open invitation. There are some common places you should look for cracks that could provide ant entry points:

- *Windows and doorframes*: These are easy entrances for ants and they're also probably the easiest places to find cracks and patch them. Seal off any crevices with silicone caulk or insulation or whatever makes sense for that particular spot. If you don't think you see any cracks, wait until night, then turn on bright lights in the room or foyer, or shine a spotlight directly on a window or doorframe from the inside. Go outside and look for places where the light shines through. Once you direct an outdoor light onto the window in order to see the caulking job, you may not be able to find all these cracks and crevices—but you will be able to get many of them.

- *Water and utility lines*: Holes where water pipes enter your home are particularly attractive to ants. Not only are the cracks around them rather large, but the water pipes also often create moisture from condensation, which itself attracts ants. They can also easily tightrope across utility lines, finding the trail's end inside your house. Get that caulking gun out again and seal around these areas, stuff insulation into the particularly large ones, or use rings with rims or rubber gaskets specially made to cover these pipe holes. This is an easy task unless your pipe and utility lines enter the house in hard-to-reach places.

Bringing Them In

Don't unwittingly carry ants into your house! Check over any houseplants that you buy or any plants that you are bringing in for wintering over, either into the house itself or into a three-season porch attached to the house. These plants can easily host a few ants. And they won't stay still for long. Soon they'll explore their new surroundings after the trip inside, especially after they warm up.

The same goes for firewood. Don't plop enough wood to last for a couple weeks down beside the fireplace. Only bring in as much as you are going to burn fairly quickly—just enough for one evening is ideal. Ants and wood go together like soup and a sandwich. Firewood that has been stacked and sitting around for most of the summer or even from the last winter is surely hosting plenty of spontaneous uncontained ant farms, which will send their denizens into your house if brought inside.

Moisture Problems

Ants are little water-seeking missiles, detecting moisture and hunting it down. If drought conditions exist outside, they will look far and wide for water sources, and your home will provide plenty. Like any animal, water is essential to their existence. And moisture in wood starts the decaying process, making it appealing to the carpenter ant for nesting excavation. There are, unfortunately, several sites for potential moisture problems in any house.

- *Roof areas*: Leaking roofs are notoriously difficult to repair. Because of the roof's slant, a leak can originate from almost anywhere—usually far from the place where the water is coming through. Any roof leak means that water is coming in contact with wood and other building materials, making the environment appealing to ants. Keeping roofs in good repair allows the roofing material to do what it is designed to do—keep water away from wood. If you discover a leak, try to trace its source as soon as possible. Chances are the roof has already been compromised for a while by the time you actually detect a leak so don't just plop buckets under the drip and wait until you have a chance to fix it. In the meantime, the ants will come marching in.

- *Gutters*: Use and maintain your gutters. Gutters are intended to direct water away from your house, especially from the foundation. In order for them to do their job, you need to clear them of debris regularly, keep them in good repair, and make sure to aim the downspouts heading in the right direction, protruding some distance from the edge of the house.
- *Foundations*: Seal all cracks in the foundation. Grade the soil around the foundation to slope away from the house, encouraging water to run away from its foundation. Don't let leaves and other debris accumulate around the edges of your house. This traps moisture and creates convenient routes where ants can travel undetected.
- *Outdoor water spigots*: A leaking spigot provides a constant source of fresh water, moist soil, and potentially moistened wood on which ants thrive. Remember, what may be a simple drop of water to you is a small pond to the ant!
- *Attics*: We don't visit them much so we tend to forget about these areas, but attics and crawl spaces need to be properly ventilated to draw moisture out of the house and keep air circulating. They also need to be properly insu-

lated so that the moisture is being stopped by the insulation's vapor barrier, rather than seeping into the insulation itself and making it an ant haven. Be sure to pop up into the attic or crawl space at least twice a year to check for roof leaks as well.

- *Air conditioning units*: Naturally a moisture creator, a/c units—either window units or the condensers of whole-house units—can attract ants, making them perfect entry spots. Check around them often and keep the moisture level around them to a minimum.
- *Screens*: Don't put off mending holes in screens, either patch them or replace the entire screen. Ants can crawl on almost anything.

Prong Two: Don't Make Your House Appealing to Ants

"What is a crumb to you and me is a ten-day food supply to some pests."

—George Baker, Professional Pest Products

After you've sealed every crack and crevice that could serve as an ant highway, you need to look at your house's interior from an ant's perspective. No matter how careful you are in sealing the exterior, ants *will* get in. Make sure your home isn't a tempting ant bistro—when they come in, you will only deter them if your house is devoid of regular sources of food and sweet liquids. And as the quotation above states, it doesn't take much to make a feast for an ant!

Since they will be most attracted to food sources, you should spend most of your time in the kitchen. A few places to pay extra attention to are:

Cupboards

Clean cupboard surfaces regularly, wiping away spilled sugar crystals, rings of vegetable oil that run down the side of the bottle, cookie crumbs that spill out of the crinkle pack when the kids tuck the package away. Use airtight containers to store any item whose original packaging doesn't provide a secure seal. And last, keep the cupboard doors tightly closed. If the latches don't close well, consider replacing them with ones that do. Remember to check the backs and corners inside the cupboard for cracks and crevices, and seal those ant entry points.

Counters

Good housekeeping is a key defense against ant visits. Wipe counters down every time you spill food. After making lunch, clear the counter of breadcrumbs. Ants will happily collect all this for you if you don't wipe it away—what is a scrap to you is to them a week's worth of food for the next generation. And don't wipe crumbs onto the floor; ants can crawl there too! For that matter, clean your floor regularly.

Waste

Under the kitchen sink is not a good place for a garbage can; the moist environment of water pipes already attracts ants and with a garbage can right there they have food and water without having to travel far. They can also get around clandestinely, since most homeowners don't spend much time under the kitchen sink. If you collect kitchen scraps to compost, don't just throw it in a bowl beside the sink until it is full. Use a sealed container (and learn what is appropriate for garden compost material and what is not so you don't attract ants to your compost pile). Empty and clean both indoor garbage cans and the compost container often. Run the dishwasher at least once a day to keep dirty plates from spending too much time sitting in the dishwasher.

Moisture

The kitchen is an obvious place for moisture in any household. The sink, the dishwasher, even the refrigerator can be problems. Steam builds up from cooking, coffee machines leak—the possibilities are endless. Mix a great water source in a room with a great food source, and the kitchen will prove to be the site of many of your ant discoveries. Keeping moisture buildup minimal is the key. Some things you can do to cut down on moisture in your home are:

- Direct cooking steam out of the house with a range vent.
- Check regularly under the sink for leaks in pipes; if the kitchen faucet leaks, repair it as soon as possible.
- Keep tabs on those spray hoses; they are common places for unnoticed leaks.

If you eat regularly in other parts of your house, don't forget to be careful there too. Wipe off those TV trays. Don't simply knock crumbs onto the living room or den floor. If you have a breakfast nook, be sure the drops of jam or honey or spilled sugar crystals are wiped away. Regularly vacuum any eating area. If you eat breakfast in bed every day or enjoy midnight snacks of crackers and cheese, well, just thinking about having ants in your bed should deter you from indulging in this regularly!

Prong Three: Indoor Chemical Pest Control

Okay, the ants are in. Although the chances are low that you are facing the type of infestation described earlier—there are no Argentine ants pouring out of your purse—you *are* seeing ants regularly. You can't leave your breakfast plate on the counter for ten minutes without finding ants slurping up the syrupy leftovers of your pancakes. They disappear around the corner of the sugar container just as you open the cupboard door. Or maybe you have a significant carpenter ant problem, which we will discuss in further detail later in this chapter.

Whatever the level of your ant visitations, you want them out. Gone. You are ready to serve up a chemical feast—and you promise that when they are gone you will do all of the things mentioned so far in this chapter to keep them away and reduce the need for using chemicals ever again. We will go into the specific pesticides and their use in further detail in Chapter Six, but let's first talk about how to know when to bring out the big guns and when to call in a professional.

Exterminator or Self-Help Pesticides?

How do you know when to use an exterminator or just go for the do-it-yourself, over-the-counter pesticides sold in your grocery store one aisle over from the cookies? Ever use the little six-pack of goo-filled cups that you place in a few strategic spots, and bye-bye anties? Or the spray can full of ant-be-gone that blasts them in their tracks?

If you are noticing just a few ants, the goo-filled cups might work fine. The idea of homeowners spraying pesticides indoors is just plain scary, however. Frank Meek of Orkin Technical Services says, "Any pesticide is potentially dangerous. Don't spray your household pesticide and then set your lettuce on the counter to cut it up for dinner. It's best to leave pesticide use to the experts."

It's not just the safety issue, but also the effectiveness issue that you need to keep in mind. Pest control experts are very knowledgeable about pest habits and behavior. Trying to remedy an ant problem yourself can lead to more severe ant problems—you may kill a few ants but rather than destroying the colony, spraying in the wrong spot can simply split one colony up into two. You'll have at least as many—and potentially more—ants as before. Then, Meek explains, further pest control will be hindered, complicating your problem considerably. Something that could perhaps have been an easy fix has now become a little more complex.

The Do-It-Yourself Route

Let's face it; you are going to try, at least once, to outwit ants on your own. Maybe you already have and you want to know what you did wrong. There are a few off-the-shelf pesticides sold regularly for ant control purposes:

- *Sprays:* The names are familiar to us all—Raid, Ortho, Safer. Many come in cans with wide-mouth sprayers and show pictures of insects upside down with Xs for eyes. For wasps and stinging bees, the sprayer claims long-range reach. For ants, it may mention that it is especially good at penetrating cracks and crevices. If you choose to use these products, be sure to take suitable precautions for working with pesticides. First and foremost, read the directions on the package and follow them to the word. If they say to ventilate the room during or after spraying, then be sure to ventilate the room. It simply isn't worth it to take chances. Likewise, if it recommends a certain amount of coverage, follow that recommendation, or you may be spraying just enough to build up the ants' resistance but not enough to kill them.

Most sprays do not have residual effects—that is, they work only when they are sprayed and perhaps for a few hours after, but their chemical compounds break down after a period of time, bringing their toxicity level down. Yet it doesn't pay to take chances—remove children and their toys, pets and their food bowls, your own dishes, and exposed food from the area you will be spraying. Wear gloves when spraying to avoid getting any pesticide on your skin. Protect your eyes, too. Again, it simply doesn't pay to take chances with pesticides.

- *Baits*: Baiting is an essential tool used extensively by pest control experts. The premise is to tempt ants to eat a substance that contains a poison. The poison needs to release slowly enough that they don't die before returning to the nest and sharing the wealth. Ideally, they are loyal workers who share their food with the queen, which proves the most successful attack of all. Once the queen in a colony or satellite colony is killed, the colony is doomed. No more offspring, no more motivation.

  Over-the-counter baits come in cup-like containers that hold just enough bait for a few weeks of control. They will take care of your run-of-the-mill minor ant problems if you are lucky enough to place them in the right spots. They're available as little metal containers with holes in the sides or as flat plastic things that resemble the little rubber cushions you put under chair legs to protect wood floors. They are so lightweight it's hard to believe there is anything in them at all.

These bait containers are not intended to hold dead ants. They contain insecticide-tainted food that lures ants into snacking on them. Then two things lead to their demise:

1. They run a pheromone trail back to the nest, alerting other foraging members of the colony to the great new lunch counter that opened.

2. They bring back some of the toxic food and spread it around by feeding it to their colony-mates.

Calling in the Pros

If you're inclined to try solving most home problems by yourself, then you will most likely take the do-it-yourself route for pest control as well. But maybe you're the type who would just as soon leave pest control to the professionals. If that is the case, there are many ways of finding a reliable extermination company.

So far, despite the widespread use of the Internet, there is still the good old-fashioned phone book. In it you will find national companies like Orkin and Terminix, and you will find local pest control companies. The national companies all have Web sites (and many of the local companies do as well) where you can get a sense of how they approach pest control. If you decide to go with one of the big guys, give their 800-number a call. They're big enough and old enough to have established strong reputations for having all the proper licenses and for training their field technicians to use toxins correctly. There's an alphabet soup of federal regulating organizations and laws and oversight organizations—the EPA, the FIFR Act, NCAMP, to name just a few—that tell them exactly how and when a certain product can be used. But the small guys are just as subject to these restrictions and regulations, too, and won't be in business long if they don't follow them.

If you are prone to extensively researching any company before you use them—which is highly recommended when choosing someone to spray toxic chemicals around your house—contact the Better Business Bureau and find out if the company has been subject to fines and other problems involving the inappropriate use of chemicals. Definitely call the Better Business Bureau to check local exterminators who don't have a national reputation to uphold—not that they would be more inclined to be less ethical, they just don't have the general ear of the consumer and the media reporting on their every false move. Ask your friends, family, and colleagues if anyone has direct experience with your local companies and ask what that experience was like.

Questions to Ask a Prospective Extermination Service

Like everything else you purchase, it pays to be a smart shopper when it comes to hiring a pest control expert. Some questions will get you the info you need in order to make an informed decision. Many of these aren't much different from things you would ask about any service company you are hiring. Here are some starters:

How long have they been in business?

Quite simply, the longer a company has been in business the more experience they have with pest control and the more chance they've had to prove their ethics and their track record with the proper use of pesticides. The larger companies also have the resources to keep up with all the latest pesticide regulations and innovations, and to extensively train their staff. If a pest control company is fairly new, that doesn't mean its owner is also new to the pest control business, so you might want to check into the professional background of the owner or the employees.

What is their overall approach to pest control?

Make sure their approach meshes with yours. If you are the kind that shops for organic produce and picks the aphids off your garden plants by hand, you probably won't be happy with a pest control company who rushes over and sprays stuff everywhere. Or maybe you simply want them to get their butts over to your house and make these ants go away no matter what it takes. Even if you are the more organic type, perhaps the invasion has gotten so out of hand that you're resigned to the pesticide route. Just know ahead of time what you are up against. Ask what they know about the safety of the chemicals they are using. If a pest control "expert" comes into your home and says things like "Well, the EPA doesn't approve this for use on ants, but we have found it to be extremely effective," fire them on the spot. There's actually little chance that you will hear this kind of thing; if an extermination company is caught using a pesticide for any uses other than those very specifically pointed out on the label, it will cost them a lot of money, if not the entire business. Frank Meek of Orkin Exterminating Company, Inc., explains, "if the label says 'crack and crevice application', and you put it on the baseboards, you've broken the law."

Do they follow up on their work?

You want a pest control company that is in it for the long haul. Although they will certainly try to sell you what basically amounts to a subscription service, you really do want someone who comes into the situation looking at a long-term plan for elimination and prevention of reinfestation. But you also don't want them to indiscriminately spray every three or four weeks—their "subscription" service should include regular visits to check on the situation and determine if spraying is called for or not.

Do they inspect your house and offer suggestions for controlling future infestations?

You want someone who will point out the weak areas that are making your home a nice place for pests. Maybe it's as simple as re-thinking your approach to kitchen waste. Or maybe it's as complex as hiring a home repair service to seal the exterior. But you are paying them to help you reduce your house's ant population, and if you knew all the preventive measures, you wouldn't be calling *them.* Any pest control company who's been in the business any length of time has seen a lot—expect them to use their experience and knowledge to help you solve your problem.

How long may it be before the ants return?

If you're having a persistent problem, be sure the exterminator tells you when you might expect a re-visit from the ants. If the next visitation comes far before the suggested amount of time, call them up and let them know.

Why Do Ants Come In?

For millions of years, ants never saw a human house and they survived just fine. Why the sudden interest in houses? *Because they're there.* Ants and most insects have survived for eons because they're not only adaptable but also often almost *immediately* adaptable. When something wipes out their foraging trail, they make a new one. When disaster strikes their nest, they pack up what they can, which is a lot, and carry on, starting a new nest in a heartbeat.

So when they're out scouting around and happen upon your house, they just keep scouting. Often, as we have seen already, what they find is quite tempting—moisture-laden wood for excavation, cracks in foundations for easy entry, and water and food somewhere down the road.

Sometimes ants are driven inside by conditions outside. Homeowners in colder climates know that once temperatures drop, many creatures seek out warmer winter homes. Ladybugs gather in the corner of the living room window to take advantage of the heat. Bats may head to the small space between your house and window shutters to hang out for a while. And some ants will find your house snug as a bug. Or should I say snug *for* a bug?

Another condition that drives ants into houses is drought. The moisture generated by a human household provides great relief for many pest ants during dry times. While termites burrow deeper into the ground, ants start swarming around water sources such as air conditioners, condensating water pipes, and leaky water spigots.[31]

So even if you don't have an ant problem right now, if you don't repair leaks and block entry points, you are a prime target for invasion the moment conditions in and around your house become more favorable than those outside.

Things to Know for Effective Ant Control

Only killing ants you can see still leaves a scent trail for all the others to follow, so here's what you need to know:

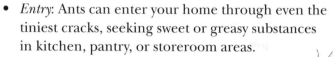

- *Entry:* Ants can enter your home through even the tiniest cracks, seeking sweet or greasy substances in kitchen, pantry, or storeroom areas.
- *Scent trails:* Ants leave a long-lasting invisible pheromone trail for the rest of the colony to follow once they locate a food source.
- *Nest locations:* They can nest about anywhere in and around your home; in lawns, walls, stumps, even under foundations.
- *Colony size:* A colony may contain 300,000 to 500,000 individuals and whole colonies can uproot and relocate quickly when threatened.
- *Nature's way of protecting the colony:* With comparative freedom from natural enemies, a colony can have a relatively long life. Worker ants may live seven years and the queen may live as long as fifteen.

(Reprinted by permission of Orkin Exterminating Company, Inc.)

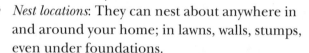

Nesting

Most ants that enter your home are simply foraging for food. Their nests are outside and your house happens to be within foraging range. They're tempted by easy entry points, the promise of moisture and warmth, and then, *voila!* they find last night's dinner plates on the counter. Then they go back and alert their friends. And if last night's dinner plates are on the counter regularly, they do the same thing you do when you find a good restaurant—they make regular visits.

But some ants will also nest in your home. Among these home-busters can be crazy ants, odorous house ants, pavement ants, pharaoh ants, and thief ants, but carpenter ants are certainly the most notorious for making your home their home. What are the traits of these invaders that attract them to your home?

Crazy Ants

Crazy ants come in, especially in the North, because they simply can't stand cold temperatures. Therefore, when they're in your house, you'll probably find them nesting near heat sources such as hot-water pipes and furnaces.[32] But like all ants, crazy ants will also enter a home when their natural food supply is reduced by outdoor conditions. Crazy ants derived their common name from their habit of wildly running around searching for food. Once they have it, you can trace them back to their nest. Or at least you can try . . .

Odorous House Ants

These smelly little ants are found throughout the U.S. Cold temperatures also drive odorous house ants inside. They too

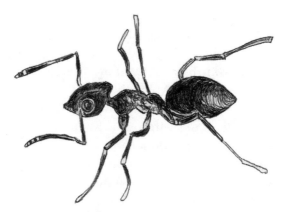

An odorous house ant.

congregate around heat sources. An odorous house ant, however, doesn't have the haphazard movement of the crazy ant,
and it will travel around your home in search of food in a much
more organized fashion.

Pavement Ants

Pavement ants are typically, as might be expected, outdoor ants
that nest in cracks in pavement. But given adverse outdoor conditions and/or agreeable indoor conditions, they will nest in
ground-level masonry walls such house foundations.[33]

They will happily use your plumbing to climb to your upper
floors. A distinguishing physical trait of the pavement ant is a set
of grooves in the head and thorax, which makes it increasingly
clear why a magnifying lens is critical to identification!

Pharaoh Ants

Another ant found throughout the U.S. is the pharaoh ant. The
NPCA Field Guide to Structural Pests lists several distinguishing
physical characteristics, one of which is a twelve-segmented antenna with a three-segmented club on the end. They live in
huge colonies, eat just about anything, and are quite adept at
traveling around your home. "Nests are usually located in inac-
cessible areas such as wall voids, behind baseboards, in furniture, under floors, and between linens. . . . They commonly use
electrical and telephone wires as a highway system to travel
through walls and between floors."[34]

This is one of the species that, as Frank Meek of Orkin describes above, readily splits a colony up into two separate
colonies if just a section, rather than the whole colony, is killed
by pesticides.

The NPCA manual explains that during the week or so it takes for the two colonies to reorganize, the homeowner thinks she has solved the problem because there is no visible activity. It soon becomes apparent, however, that the pest problem not only remains, but it's also worse. Pharaoh ants are a tough bunch to get a handle on once they're entrenched, and they're recognized disease carriers. Pest control professionals not only highly recommend that homeowners do not take these pests on themselves, but they also say that once the extermination procedure is in place, it is critical that homeowners do not disturb it.

Thief Ants

Since thief ants get their name from the habit of nesting near or even in the nests of other ants, it seems logical that, if you are working at controlling one kind of ant, you are probably trying to control these as well. Their colonies are not very large, and they are found throughout the country. As innocuous as they might be for other reasons, since they feed on dead rats and mice, they should still be considered possible disease carriers.[35]

Carpenter Ants

These little guys always deserve a lengthy discussion because they do much more than simply visit your home to feast on a breadcrumb or syrup puddle or a few sugar crystals. While most ants are just pests, carpenter ants pose a real threat to your house's well-being. They will eat away at it, sometimes doing so undetected for months. Be diligent when it comes to carpenter ants; the structural damage they inflict can be costly to repair since it is often in hard-to-reach places.

Carpenter ants are found throughout the U.S. The black carpenter ant (*Camponotus pennsylvanicus*) is the species common in the eastern U.S. The western version (*C. modoc*) is mostly black with reddish legs and golden hairs on its abdomen (detectible if you get up close with a magnifying glass). Carpenter ants don't sting, but they can inflict a painful bite since they inject formic acid.

A bright side to carpenter ant control is their colonies' moderate population size—averaging between 3,000 and 15,000 workers including satellite colonies—and that there is only one queen per colony. Meaning if you find a nest and destroy it, you have destroyed the queen and don't have to wonder how many other queens there are left in other non-visible locations.

Carpenter ants don't forage too far from the nest—they stick to around 300 feet. Their preferred foods are honeydew from other insects, plant and fruit juices, and other insects. They also eat sweets, eggs, meats, and grease.[36]

Moisture control is the most important line of defense against carpenter ants. They rarely tackle sound wood for their nests, but go for any mushy, water-softened support beam or

Carpenter ants will feed each other.

plank in your house. Locating the nest is the key to solving an existing carpenter ant problem.

One way to locate carpenter ants is by looking for an accumulation of sawdust and other debris at the base of the openings they are working on. These ants are very meticulous in their housekeeping, pushing all the excess sawdust from their tunnels and all other junk out of the nest.

They also make quite a lot of noise while doing their excavation work, which typically takes place at night in a dark and otherwise quiet home. Nighttime is the best time to check the perimeters of your foundation because this is when the ants will be the most active. If you follow them, you may be able to home in on their nest.

Listening devices such as a stethoscope can help determine their presence—if you find a suspicious area, tap it with a screwdriver and listen for a change in the sounds. Also, a moisture meter can lead you to likely places for a colony's nest since moisture is so key to where they decide to settle down.

You'll also know you have carpenter ants if you see them swarm. In order for this to happen, the nest has to be at least two years old. Swarming—flying together in large groups, either during mating or while changing nest sites when starting a new colony, or when the nest has been disturbed—can be observed from May to August in the East and February through June in the West. Basically, you will be tipped off to their presence when you see winged ants in your home.

Once you find a carpenter ant nest—which will probably require the help of a professional exterminator who knows all the clues—its destruction is relatively simple and effective. Typically, the exterminator dusts or sprays the nest with an insecticide. Treatment is usually location-specific; however, it may be necessary to inject insecticide into the surrounding wall areas to ensure complete elimination. Again, only a professional pest control expert can best determine the need for a more widespread application and will save your home from excess insecticide use.

After the nest has been successfully exterminated, be sure to repair the damaged area. Then go back to the moisture-control prevention measures and seal your home against future infestations.

Where Do Ants Nest?

Ants have discovered several places in human homes that make perfect nesting sites for ant colonies. The choice of site depends on the species, and many have the luxury of choosing from several possibilities. In general, nesting sites can be in:

- *Insulation*: Anywhere in your home where there is insulation is a potential ant-nesting site, including refrigerator insulation and around air conditioning units and water heaters. Wall and attic insulation, both the batting and loose type, often harbors undetected moisture, which makes it perfect for ants. They get moisture, warmth, and fuzzy nesting material all in one spot! Whether the insulation fibers make them itch or not . . .

- *Wall voids*: Pest control literature frequently mentions "wall voids" as good places for ants to nest. This is the space between the outside wall of your home—usually wood boards or plywood—and the wall that makes up the living space, which is usually plaster or drywall.

These two walls leave a nice cavity in between them that most likely contains insulation. That's okay by the ant, though, since as mentioned above, the insulation itself makes ideal nesting material.

- *Foundations:* Nesting near house foundations is commonplace for some ants, leaving them within foraging range of your kitchen, to which they will surely have established a scent trail.
- *Seldom-used items:* Things that you put in storage in the garage or on the porch or in the attic are nesting targets since they go undisturbed for long periods of time. Don't think just clothing or other fabrics; also think books and paper goods.

What to Do Until the Pest Control Expert Comes

Pest control experts obviously exterminate any pests causing you problems, but before they can do that they need to accomplish the sometimes-complex task of identifying the pest and locating the nest. Their access to scientific research and experience in the field points them to the methods that will create the most effective overall plan for elimination and prevent further infestation.

Identification

Exterminators have various tools at their disposal that enable them to properly identify which pest is perpetrating crimes in your home. Of course, the difference between an ant and a rodent infestation is typically self-evident. But when it comes to differentiating between, say, ants and termites, or even different ant species, the task gets a little more complicated. For instance, Frank Meek of Orkin Exterminating Company, Inc., says that in the southern states the Allegheny mound ant and the Florida carpenter ant are almost identical in appearance. But once you can positively identify which ant you are looking at, Meek explains, you look for its nest in different places. For the carpenter ant, Meek would head to places with insulation, while for the Allegheny mound ant, he would look outside under debris attractive to the species.

Still, a simple thirty-power hand-held magnifying lens is one of the most useful tools in the field. Termites and winged ants can look quite similar to the layperson's naked eye. But up close these creatures have three features that immediately distinguish them from one another to the trained observer:

1. The ant has the classic narrow waist distinguishing it from other insects of the Hymenoptera order.
2. Ant antennae have an elbow and the termite's do not.
3. The wings of the ant do not have as many veins running through them as the termite's and, although both have two sets of wings, the rear set of the ant's wings are smaller than the front ones. The termite's four wings are about equal in size.

Identifying pests using a microscope or hand-held lens and a pictorial key allows the exterminator, says Meek, to know where to go to look for entry points and/or nests, and how to proceed with elimination.

Collect a Specimen or Two

Exterminators are busy people, and it may be a day or two before someone can get to your house. And when they finally show up, the ants may decide they don't feel like coming out for examination. Meek suggests doing the following three things until the pest control expert gets there:

- First and foremost, don't spray anything. You will definitely make the exterminator's job more difficult and, as mentioned above, you might make the situation more complex than it was before you sprayed.
- Second, collect a few specimens of the pest since they may not be visible at the exact time the exterminator arrives. "*Don't,*" Meek warns, "stick your specimen onto a piece of paper with tape." In order to identify the ant, he needs to be able to roll it around and look at various identification points. Instead, get a small medicine vial or a film canister and put a little rubbing alcohol in it. Moisten a cotton ball or cotton swab, press it gently on the ant until the ant sticks to the cotton, and put it in vial. Collect two or three to make sure you have one that is in identifiable condition. "We spend lots of time with diagnosis," Meek explains, and the first step is identification.
- Third, go ahead and remove food and water sources that the ants are clearly using as they raid your house on foraging missions.

How Do Ants Get In?

Ants aren't out in the dark of night with a flashlight looking for gaps around the windows or crevices that would allow them to sneak into the basement. Most likely, they are attracted to some area of your house that has a moisture problem. Once there, they may forage around and in their wanderings, find themselves inside. Once they find a food source, you're on their shopping list. Some common places ants may make grand entrances are:

- Cracks and crevices in the foundation.
- Electrical and communications lines that conveniently run through a hole from the outside to the inside of your house.
- Gaps around the point where water pipes enter the house.
- Cracks and crevices around window and doorframes.
- Hitchhiking on logs intended for your fireplace.

And Then There Were None

You will never get rid of every ant in and around your house—and you don't want to! It would be an ominous sign of a very off-balance environment if there were no ants anywhere. But you should be able to keep in check the number of ants frolicking around your kitchen quite often all on your own with the occasional assistance from a pest control expert for the most extreme and persistent cases.

5

Ants in the Yard and Garden

Usually, an indoor ant problem really means an outdoor ant problem. Most ants don't want to live in your home. In fact, they don't typically live there at all—the ants you see scrounging around your kitchen counters and scurrying across the floor are usually workers, out on food-gathering missions. Their colony's nest is probably located near your house, within foraging range, and unless you've paid special attention to making your home less ant-accessible, entry is easy. And unless you've paid special attention to making your home less ant-friendly, food sources abound.

With the exception of fire ants, most ants are fairly innocuous when outside. If you can keep their colonies within a reasonable distance from your house, they will definitely do more good than harm. Their foraging area is not that wide, usually just a few yards but it can range as far as several hundred yards from the nest. They will continue to return to the same spot where they found food as long as they continue to find food there. Typically, they then tell their foraging worker nest mates and ultimately become what we humans call an ant problem.

There are several things you can do to make the area immediately surrounding your house uninteresting to ants of most kinds. Also, understanding why ants may seek out your house and other buildings can help you understand how to avoid or control ant invasions.

Weather and Climate Conditions

As much as we humans have tried, we cannot control the weather. Nonetheless, you can pay attention to climate conditions that may drive ants into your house. They react to severe and unusual weather just like we do. You might never have had an ant problem before but some climactic anomaly one summer can change all that in a heartbeat.

During droughts, they look for water sources. As mentioned above and in the previous chapter, houses typically offer many potential water sources for ants—air conditioning units, condensation on water pipes, or leaking water spigots exiting the foundation.

Excess water, such as an extended rainy season, will also drive ants indoors looking for relief from flooding nests. Or they may just want to search for food without drowning.

Long hot spells are also hard on ants. They may seek the cool shade of your foundation, and then your basement. Next, they find that there is food in the kitchen, and the invasion begins.

Climactic conditions can change the way that pest control experts handle baiting, too. In an article describing ant invasions during a summer drought in Virginia, exterminators said, "liquid baits are working better than solid ones, because the ants are so thirsty."[37] If you don't want to bother with the details of why ants do what they do under every condition, consider calling a pest control expert who has experience with all those things.

Trees

"Trees," says Orkin's Frank Meek, "are the biggest problem. This is also one where it is hardest to get homeowners to cooperate. Trees create avenues and food sources, or they lead to other avenues like utility lines that run through trees."

If you want to reduce your ant problems, be a cooperative homeowner. Inspect your yard for potential tree problems. Deciduous trees are great natural heating and cooling partners—planted strategically, they can shade your home in the summer when their leaves are abundant and allow the sun to come through in the winter when the tree is bare. But plant them with ant control in mind, and inspect them a couple times a year with an eye toward appropriately pruning.

Of course, you can always resort to insecticides and those sticky traps and tapes that combat ants in trees—the tape can be wrapped around the diameter of the trunk to provide a barrier that ants cannot pass. At least they won't go beyond them until so many ants are trapped on the sticky tape that newcomers can just walk over dead and dying bodies to get to the other side without touching the sticky stuff. These sticky tapes are about as environmentally friendly as you can get; there are no pesticides on them; they're just gooey. Yet trapping ants in place and letting them die of starvation and dehydration seems to be cruel and unusual punishment. But if killing the ants is the best solution for your problem, there are lots of methods mentioned in Chapter Seven on "natural" and low-toxic pest controls that can deliver swift death or at least strong discouragement. If you practice serious prevention, however, the trees and ants can live in harmony.

First and foremost, don't let tree branches touch your house. The trees themselves don't cause ant problems, but ants travel through trees all the time. If they can walk off a branch and onto your house without skipping a beat, they do. And if they are walking around on your house they will probably find an entrance, especially if there are enticingly large gaps near moist areas. Once they enter, they will probably find *some* food that appeals to them, target your house as a reliable food source, string one of their pheromone trails back to the nest, and *voila,* your house has a "New Restaurant Open: Ants Welcome" sign hanging on it.

Trees touching your house are not the only direct entrances ants use. Tree limbs overhanging the house that are a short drop to the roof also provide easy access. And, as Frank Meek points out, trees with utility lines running through them afford indirect access—the ants climbing on the trees also find themselves on a utility line that conveniently runs right to your house, which has a gap where the line goes inside that is plenty big enough for them to crawl through without having to so much as duck. So when the utility company comes by and wants to trim the trees along the road, say "yes," and be thankful that someone else is outwitting ants for you.

There are other things to keep in mind besides trimming trees away from houses, though. If you cut a tree down—for whatever reason—chop it up, remove it as soon as possible, and have the stump removed as well. Stumps are tempting sites for ants to team up and expedite the decaying process. In the middle of the forest, this is a good thing; but whenever you encourage ants to live close to your house, you are inviting a potential invasion.

Also, repair damaged or diseased trees near your house or other outbuildings. Decay attracts ants (especially carpenter ants that nest or burrow in the dead portions of trees, stumps, and logs), and therefore encourages them to be close enough to your house to be problems. Remove the stumps, dying trees, and logs before they become ant havens.

Firewood

As mentioned in an earlier chapter, keep firewood away from buildings. To discourage nest building in firewood stacks, get your cordwood up off the ground. Use it up quickly, especially the wood that you bring into the house for use in the fireplace or woodstove. Bring in wood that you're not planning to burn immediately and you may have just helped an ant colony move into your house. Check wood after it has been sitting in your house for a while to see if ants have started to move about after getting warmed up a little.

Ants Love Aphids

In and of themselves, ants in the vegetable garden don't represent much of a hazard. Where there is an abundance of ants in a garden, however, there is almost certainly an abundance of aphids. And aphids spell trouble for many garden plants, flowers, and fruit trees. They'll feed on juices from plants, harming the plants in the process. Leaves and buds grow deformed, wilt, and brown. They are then less able to produce fruit vigorously and become susceptible to diseases, pests, and other hazards that befall weakened plants.

Ants and aphids have a very complex relationship that has been well studied. Aphids produce a liquid called "honeydew," of which ants are particularly fond. (Except for Z, the ant in the movie *AntZ*, who is discontent with his lot in life. In one scene Z, whose voice is that of Woody Allen, sits in a bar with his worker pals. When offered a "honeydew beer," he rejects it. "Call me crazy but I have a thing about drinking from the anus of another creature," he says.) This is exactly what ants do—they tap the abdomen of the aphid with their antennae, which stimulates the aphid to produce the liquid.

To support their habit, as explained in more detail in Chapter Three, ants actually take care of aphids as a farmer would a herd of milk cows. In return for the honeydew sustenance, ants protect aphids from many of their enemies, even killing their predators. Ants have been observed moving aphids around to more protected or hospitable places when conditions are less than perfect for their "cows." So, although ants themselves don't have a huge impact on your garden, they'll harbor the more destructive aphids.

Where you see an abundance of ants, look for aphid infestations in the form of clusters of tiny green, red, brown, or black insects on the undersides of leaves, especially new growth, in your garden. You can simply hose them off with water or spray soapy water or insecticidal soap to kill them. Ladybugs and lacewings are effective biological controls for aphids and ants. Plowing the soil in your garden in the fall will expose and kill aphid eggs left to overwinter. Planting mints, tansy, and pennyroyal throughout the garden will also help repel aphids during the growing season.

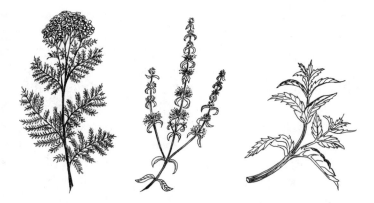

Tansy, spearmint, and pennyroyal are all natural ant repellents.

If you didn't manage to till in the fall, or even if you did, you can repeatedly till the soil deeply in the early spring to try to get rid of the aphids before you begin to plant the year's crops. Good soil management, which includes monitoring nutrient levels, is key since aphids tend to attack weak plants.

Aphids don't just feed on vegetable garden plants. They can also be found in trees, shrubs, and flowers that you plant close to your house. When you find a significant ant population, investigate for aphids, because until the aphids are eliminated you will probably have little luck removing the ants.

Biological Controls

Lacewings (Neuroptera) come in brown or green and get their common name from their large transparent wings that have a lacy network of veins spreading throughout them. Green lacewings, which range in color from pale green to brilliant green, lay eggs on leaves near aphids. The larvae eat anything they can get a hold of (including each other) when they emerge from the eggs, so aphids beware—each larva can devour hundreds of aphids before it reaches adulthood!

Lacewings can be found throughout North America and can be bought as eggs for use in the garden.

Tiger beetles (Cicindelidae) prey on ants. And many species of ladybugs (or, more correctly, lady beetles) prey on aphids.

Plants That Attract Beneficial Insects

There are many plants that you can grow near your home and garden that will attract ant predators like ladybugs and lacewings to your environs: alfalfa, angelica, carrot, evergreen euonymus, goldenrod, oleander, ragweed, and yarrow. To repel ant-attracting aphids, try planting onions and garlic. On the other hand, plants from the Aster and Parsley families may lead aphid-eaters to your garden.[38]

Other Garden Suggestions

Many flowers are susceptible to aphid infestations, which makes them just as susceptible to ant infestations since we now know how important the aphid is to the ant. As with most things involving pests, prevention is the key to outwitting them. Here are some tips to keep in mind:

- Always buy healthy plants. Plants that are sickly may already be infested with pests such as aphids, and, if not, will be much more susceptible.
- Do not take cuttings from diseased or sickly plants. You're just asking for further diseased and frail plants in the future.
- Help plants get a healthy start. Put them in places that are best suited to their needs. Prepare the soil properly and make sure it's nourished with all the nutrients the plant needs to thrive.
- Don't space plants as young seedlings in a way that will cause overcrowding when they are mature. Overcrowding is another direct route to unhealthiness because there will not be enough nutrients, air, sunshine, and water to go around.
- Spend some quality time with your plants. Inspect them for disease and pests. Prune and weed as necessary. Look for insect damage such as buds that don't develop, browning or withered leaves, twisted stems and leaves, or otherwise deformed foliage and flowers.

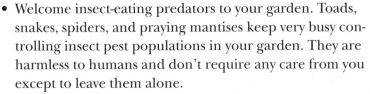

- Welcome insect-eating predators to your garden. Toads, snakes, spiders, and praying mantises keep very busy controlling insect pest populations in your garden. They are harmless to humans and don't require any care from you except to leave them alone.
- Encourage bird visits. Hang feeders near your garden and plant shrubs and trees that attract birds. Most birds eat ants, and many eat aphids as well.
- If you must use insecticides to rid plants of aphids, and therefore ants, be sure to keep in mind that the insecticides are not selective and will kill beneficial insects as well, such as lacewings and ladybugs. Spray in the evening after the bees have gone to bed. Try to direct the spray as carefully as possible to keep from broadcasting it to other plants and insects.
- Plant bug-repellent plants, including marigolds, alliums, evening primroses, baby blue eyes, candytuft, tansy, bishop's flowers, black-eyed Susans, pennyroyal, strawflowers, nasturtiums, angelica, yarrow, and many mints.

Lawns

Harvester ants feed on grasses and have occasionally been known to be a real problem in lawns. They can be recognized by the ring of seed husks around their nest opening. Pavement ants are often found nesting in lawns. Mounds are perhaps the most serious problem created by ants in lawns, making mowing difficult.

Mulching

Mulching is usually good for plants, but mulches can attract ants by keeping soil moist and cool, and by making a nice place to set up summer homes. Keep this in mind when mulching shrubs and trees that are near the house.

Specific Species

Most species of pest ants are active both indoors and out, but they do differ significantly in their tendency to actually invade our houses. Often the key to whether an ant species will come inside or not is its dependency on honeydew and other sweet-liquid food sources. If these sources—especially aphids—disappear from the environment, either from natural causes or through pest control, the ant will look indoors to satisfy its sweet tooth.

Fire Ants

The fire ant poses the most serious outdoor ant problem. Their notorious stings and bites require caution while outside in most warm areas of the U.S. They typically nest in the ground, sometimes next to building foundations. Fire ants do not feed on honeydew; instead, they feed directly on plants—destroying many of them in the process.

Fire ants should be taken seriously. Their infestations can be huge—in one acre, there may be as many as a thousand mounds, each containing several hundred thousand stinging ants.[39] And they protect themselves and their nests with vigor. The sting of one lone fire ant is incomparable to the pain of a wasp or bee sting, but that one fire ant can—and will—sting several times as well as bite. They are also invariably joined by hundreds of their friends and kin before the biting and stinging begins.

The Colorado State University "Fire Ants" fact sheet says that in infested areas, it is almost impossible to avoid stepping on a mound or on the tunnels they build, which they also protect ferociously. The national parks system has a complex job dealing with fire ant populations since heavy use of insecticides would also have serious impact on other species and habitats.

Fire ants in the yard are not welcome visitors. Although, in general, fire ants are nuisance pests, children and pets are particularly vulnerable. They can be seriously injured or even die from an attack. Therefore, calling in pest control professionals makes sense when dealing with these ants. Professionals have access to and expertise with appropriate pesticides. They can also effectively and strategically use bait controls, which take longer to significantly affect an entire colony yet don't broadcast pesticides all over your yard.

Fire ants are not typically indoor pests, but they occasionally go inside to seek shade and coolness as other ants do when outdoor conditions become unbearable. If you suspect fire ants have entered your home, call pest control experts immediately.

Argentine Ants

Argentine ants build their shallow nests where they find moisture: under boards and stones, beneath plants, and along sidewalks. When the weather turns dry (or even too wet), they will head indoors. Argentine ants are also honeydew-eaters, which means that when honeydew is low, they may turn up in your kitchen searching for sweets.

Carpenter Ants

Carpenter ants nest outside in any wood, including rotting fence posts, stumps, old firewood, dead portions of standing trees, and under stones or fallen logs. They forage up to 300 feet from their nest, cutting a clear path across lawns.

As has been outlined in other chapters, carpenter ants, along with fire ants are cause for concern. The fire ant has a vicious bite and painful sting. But carpenter ants can cause extensive structural damage to your house and do so for a long time before they're detected. Follow all of the guidelines mentioned above for firewood storage, fixing and preventing moisture leaks in structures and around foundations, and creating an uninviting and inhospitable home for these destructive ants.

Outside, however, carpenter ants perform a necessary function of accelerating the decomposition of dead wood and other decaying matter.

Crazy Ants

The crazy ant is another ant that may invade your house when honeydew supplies are low—usually in the fall or after a rain. They build shallow outdoor nests in soil under objects, or they search out cozy cavities. Look for them in plants and trees, trash, refuse, mulch, and in potted plants.

Little Black Ants

These little mostly innocuous ants nest under stones and rocks outside, as well as in rotting logs or lawns. They are commonly seen scurrying along foundations or along sidewalks. Those common little volcano-like craters of fine churned-up soil that spills out around a little opening are sure signs that little black ants are in your neighborhood.

Odorous House Ants

According to the NPCA, these ants are extremely reliant on honeydew and when the supply is interrupted, they go in desperate search of replacement food sources. They are commonly found in your house, but their nest is most likely outside or perhaps near the foundation or under an object. They also make themselves at home in the nests of larger ants.

Pavement Ants

True to their names, these ants are found nesting under hard things such as stones, cracks in pavement, and near foundations of buildings. They forage only for a distance of around thirty feet, and they also make themselves at home in lawns.

Pharaoh Ants

Although pharaoh ants can nest in lawns and gardens (look for them in hidden or well-protected areas), these cold-sensitive ants cannot survive outdoors in temperate or northern areas of the U.S. They may survive year round, however, in the subtropical climates of Florida and Hawaii.

Thief Ants

These tiny ants are found in a variety of outdoor locations: in exposed soil or under objects, in trash, rotten wood, and cavities in trees. They often build nests under rocks.

Velvety Tree Ants

According to the *NPCA Field Guide to Structural Pests*, this is your picnic pest. They nest under stones and in hollow sections of trees, and their foraging trails can range several hundred feet from the nest.

And Now for the Benefits

All ants are beneficial until humans determine them to be pests. But sometimes ants can actually serve as a biological control against other pests. For instance, several species of ant, including a relative to the big-headed ant, *Pheidole tysoni*, are natural predators of the sod webworm, the larval stage of a small tan moth. The moth is not a problem, but its larvae eat blades of grass causing brown patches in lawns, the size of which will be determined by the maturity of the larvae and how much grass they need to consume.

Many ant species are also significant predators of termites and can kill large numbers of termites in a short period of time. They eat the young of other pests such as silverfish and clothes moths, and even flea larvae. They also clean up debris from places you can't see, perhaps keeping other pests from finding them first.

6

Pesticides and Chemicals

"I am pessimistic about the human race because it is too ingenious for its own good. Our approach to nature is to beat it into submission. We would stand a better chance of survival if we accommodated ourselves to this planet and viewed it appreciatively instead of skeptically and dictatorially."

—E. B. White

My mother's parents died in the late 1990s and when my mother was preparing to sell their house, I spent some time rummaging through the garage. There were piles of greasy tools, a couple of chainsaws buried under the workbench, and a grime-coated wooden toolbox that, when cleaned up, proved to be a thing of beauty. Also buried here and there in the garage and in the basement were containers of pesticides—insecticides, herbicides, rodenticides, you name it. I was absolutely certain some of them had been banned in previous years. We put them all in a box and took them to a waste management site that accepts toxic materials for appropriate disposal.

The same thing happened when we bought our farm. The previous owner had been a man of my grandfather's vintage, and the pesticides stored in various places around the farm were of the same era as well. Off to the toxic waste disposal site they went.

Since containers of old pesticides have appeared twice in my life already, I suspect the number of similar containers out there waiting to be discovered (or worse yet, continuing to be used) is huge.

The first thing you need to keep in mind about pesticides, and in the case of ant control these would be known as insecticides, is that they are usually synthetic chemicals that are often very dangerous. Pesticides serve a great purpose in our contemporary world. Neverthless, that they should be "used with caution" is an understatement.

The History and Development of Pesticides

The use of pesticides can be traced to the time of Homer, around 1,000 B.C. Burning brimstone—what we know today as sulfur—may have been the first attempt at a fumigant insecticide. Later, historian Pliny the Elder (A.D. 23–79) listed many of the substances and methods used by ancients to control insects in his *Natural History:* the use of gall from a green lizard to protect apples from worms and rot, the extracts of pepper and tobacco, soapy water, whitewash, vinegar, turpentine, fish oil, brine, lye, and many others.[40]

Humans are not the only ones to use chemicals to combat things that bother us. Animals do it all the time and have since the beginning of creation—they exude odors and secrete liquids that repel predators or lay claim to territory or they actually inject chemicals into prey that liquefies them (they're easier to digest that way). In fact, early humans probably rubbed mud on their bodies and covered themselves in dust to detract insects, much like horses, cows, and elephants still do. Even innocuous substances like mud and dust would be considered insecticides when used for this purpose.

But we humans, ingenious as we are, create chemicals outside ourselves to use in widespread applications. Take the infamous DDT.

The "Miracle" Insecticide

The pesticide DDT (dichlorodiphenyltrichloroethane . . . *whew!*) was developed by a Swiss entomologist, Dr. Paul Müller, in 1939. This "miracle insecticide" turned out to be a Pandora's box. In the thirty-three years that it was in use, the world produced more than four billion pounds of the stuff. We sprayed it aerially; we used it to combat Dutch elm disease. By the end of World War II, it was used throughout the world to combat insect-vectored diseases: yellow fever, typhus, elephantiasis, and malaria. We were delighted with our newfound freedom from certain insects and disease carriers—until they resurfaced in droves, now resistant not only to DDT but also to the several other replacement pesticides we came up with, including chlordane, heptachlor, and benzene hexachloride. The pesticide revolution had gone a bit too far.

Controversy

If you have ever discussed or read anything about pesticides you have probably heard of Rachel Carson's book *Silent Spring*. Published in 1962, this groundbreaking work revealed to the average reader the shortsightedness of destroying the earth with indiscriminate use of deadly pesticides. Birds and fish are especially susceptible to this kind of contamination, and Carson described in detail the adverse effects they experienced. Bird populations were being decimated by ingesting chemicals that weakened the shells of the eggs produced by the females, which didn't allow young to develop to full term and hatch. Common fishways were also depleted of stock. Carson described the future as she saw it, devoid of birds, fish, and tender grasses along the roadsides. It was a bleak prediction—if we didn't stop the rampant use of deadly pesticides and recognize them for what they are besides pest killers, the world would become a barren place. In fact, pesticides would prove to kill humans as well, causing gene mutations that resulted in deadly cancers, deformities, lung diseases, heart defects, and a host of other health problems.

Humans seem to have a penchant for taking everything to the extreme, and pesticide use is no exception. Pesticide use in moderation is useful but we all need to prevent the wholesale spread of harmful chemicals.

After DDT was banned from the U.S. in the early 1970s, pesticides that are more selective were developed—ones that target specific insects rather than kill everything in their path in the manner of the broad-spectrum insecticides. The selective pesticides also tend to be biodegradable, breaking down into materials that do not pollute groundwater and soil. But these often water-based chemicals do not last as long or pack as strong a wallop as harsher chemicals. We can counteract this problem by practicing other pest management strategies in conjunction with pesticide use.

Pesticide Handling

According to the American Association of Poison Control Centers, "In 1996 alone, more than 50,000 kids under age six were involved in household pesticide poisonings or exposure." This grim statistic underscores the importance of proper pesticide handling, storage, and disposal. It should be taken seriously and performed in an appropriate manner.

Pesticides must be federally registered with the Environmental Protection Agency and at the state level. The EPA requires that pesticides registered by them must carry detailed labels that explain exactly how much, how often, where, and for what purpose the pesticide is approved for use. The label also lists the product's active ingredients and their toxicity levels.

The Extension Toxicology Network Web site is designed to answer questions that you might have about toxicants and the environment, how toxicants may affect you, and how you can become aware of possible hazards around you. It includes an extensive list of FAQs on subjects such as food safety issues, adverse health risks, and protecting pesticide-sensitive populations.

DIY

As has been emphasized in other chapters, do-it-yourself use of pesticides is not recommended. Nevertheless, if you must, be sure to:

- Ascertain not only what you are targeting (ants, termites, wasps, cockroaches) but also which species of ant you are having problems with.
- Do not put anything, no matter how safe it claims it is, within reach of children or pets.
- Wear appropriate protective clothing, gloves, masks, and headgear while using the pesticide product.
- Use the product only as specifically outlined on the label. If it says to use it for baseboard treatment, use it along baseboards only—do not use the product around outdoor lamps or in the wall voids.
- Use exactly the amount of the product that is specified on the label. Do not use more and risk overexposure, and do not use less and risk ineffectiveness.

Pest Control Experts

Exterminating companies still use plenty of pesticides to do their jobs. These days, however, educated consumers often request that pest control experts avoid the overuse of pesticide spray cans and incorporate what has become known as "integrated pest management" (IPM) into their company's practices. When searching for a pest control company, don't be so bowled over by your immediate problem that you don't ask plenty of questions regarding this important approach (read more about IPM at the end of this chapter).

Acute Toxicity

Acute toxicity is the dose level of a pesticide that causes immediate adverse effects in a human after brief exposure. This can be as simple as dizziness or nausea, and as serious as death. LC (lethal concentration) and LD (lethal dose) are two measurements that show the amount of product it takes to cause death.

Chronic Toxicity

Chronic toxicity refers to long-term symptoms and conditions after long-term exposure. These effects typically include cancer and chronic respiratory disease.

Labels

As mentioned above, labels on pesticides are required by federal and some state laws to be explicit, giving detailed information about use. On a pesticide label, you should find general information, such as how long you must wait before re-entry into the treated area, and storage and disposal requirements for the product and its empty container. Another significant portion of the label lists the ingredients and toxicity level of the product. Of course, the product name is clearly identified. And a precautionary statement, which can be lengthy, includes information about hazards to people, pets, the environment, and some basic first aid for exposure reactions, whether swallowed, breathed, or exposed to skin.

The name and location of the manufacturer should also be clearly printed on the label. If you need some specific information, contact them. Also, the label absolutely should include an EPA registration number. If it doesn't, do not use the product and call your state EPA to investigate.

Protective Gear

Wearing protective clothing and equipment is a no-brainer when it comes to handling pesticides of any kind. Never inhale the pesticide or let it come in contact with your bare skin (and certainly don't swallow it!). Cover yourself from head to toe. Wear long pants, a long-sleeved shirt, and waterproof gloves and footwear that won't readily absorb any spilled pesticide. Wear a hat, since the scalp easily absorbs pesticides. Wear eye protection and at least a simple respiratory mask.

Contaminated clothing should not just be thrown in your washer and dryer with the rest of the laundry. Hand washing it in a utility sink or basin is best. If you must use your washer, be prepared to carefully clean it (run it through a cycle with a hot setting, on the lowest water level, with detergent but no clothes). After hand- or machine-washing, dry the clothes outside—do not use your dryer.

And one last thing. Don't forget to let your neighbors know if you are planning to treat your yard with pesticides. Some people are extremely sensitive to any chemicals, pesticides or otherwise, and they can use the forewarning to shut their windows and abstain from lounging on the back deck when the spraying starts.

Two important phone numbers to keep beside your telephone for pesticide emergencies are:

- **1–800–222–1222** is a toll-free number for the American Association of Poison Control Centers.

  Call this number in a poisoning emergency for information on what to do. Have the poison container at hand so you can read the label to the operator. If the victim has collapsed or is not breathing, however, immediately call 911.

- **1–800–426–4435** is a toll-free number for the National Animal Poison Control Center.

  Call them if you suspect that a pet has gotten into a poisonous substance. They can tell you what are the signs of poisoning and what to administer as an antidote. Again, as with humans, if you know the substance your pet got into, have the container ready to read the label to the operator. If your pet is not breathing or is unconscious, bring it immediately to your veterinarian or emergency animal care center.

Pressure-treated Lumber

One common household product that has been the topic of hot debate over the past several years is pressure-treated lumber, especially when it is used for building things such as children's playground equipment.

Pressure treating is intended to prolong lumber's usefulness by lessening general decay and insect damage. A common form of pressure treating is "CCA-treating" which treats wood with chromated copper arsenicals.

A recent development has been to promote the labeling of such wood in the lumberyard. According to the EPA, CCA is a chemical mixture consisting of three pesticidal compounds: chromium, copper, and arsenic. Federal law directs the EPA to periodically review and reevaluate older pesticides to ensure that they continue to meet current safety standards. Not only is the EPA evaluating potential risks to children who play on equipment made of pressure-treated lumber, but also the potential occupational risks to workers who come in regular contact with CCA-treated wood. They are also evaluating its ability to leach into groundwater.

The National Pesticide Information Center is a cooperative effort between the EPA and Oregon State University. Their toll-free number for questions is 1–800–858–7378. The NPIC Web site (www.npic.orst.edu) contains an extensive list of pesticide manufacturers and their contact details, as well as links to pesticide information sheets and information on what to do in an emergency.

The Chemical Details

There are several categories of insecticides, which are divided by their chemical makeup.

Organochlorines

The organochlorines have largely been banned from use, with only a few still allowed in the contemporary arsenal of insecticides. These potent compounds contain carbon, hydrogen, and chlorine. DDT, the most notorious of the group, prevents the normal transmission of nerve impulses in humans and insects. "DDT jitters"—involuntary muscle twitching—precedes convulsions and death.[41]

Other organochlorines were Hexchlorocyclohexane, cyclodienes, and polychloroterpenes. Structures treated with cyclodienes chlordane and others are still protected from damage by termites more than fifty-five years later—that's potent stuff![42] Yet, this potency also made them very persistent in the environment, and they were all banned from use by the EPA in the 1970s and 1980s.

Organophosphates

Insecticides containing phosphates are referred to as organophosphates. Organophosphates have been in the news in the context of nerve gases such as sarin.

Organosulfurs

Organosulfurs have little effect on insects and, therefore, are not used in ant control.

Carbamates

The modus operandi of the carbamate class of insecticides is to inhibit the vital enzyme cholinesterase. One of the best-known carbamates is the insecticide Sevin, introduced in 1956. Carbamates, although they have a broad spectrum of insect control, have low toxicity to mammals.

Formamidines

This small group of insecticides poisons insects causing them to become inactive and die.

Dinitrophenols

Like the organochlorines, this class of pesticide has been banned from use.

Organotins

These are mostly used against mites (referred to as "acaricides") and as fungicides, but have no use in ant control.

Pyrethroids

The pyrethroids may be among the somewhat misunderstood insecticides in current popular use. Natural pyrethrum is the substance created by the chrysanthemum flower. It paralyzes insects quickly but doesn't necessarily kill them. These substances are relatively unstable and costly. In the latter part of the 1990s, synthetic pyrethrum-like materials were created called "pyrethroids." Ironically, these work on the nervous system much like DDT and are in widespread use against agricultural pests.

Nicotinoids

Nicotinoid—synthetic nicotine—is used as a soil, seed, or foliar treatment.

Benzoylureas

There are several other classes of insecticides, but the benzoylureas are of significance because they act as insect growth regulators.

Avermectins

These belong in the category of "antibiotics" and are used in fire ant baits. They block neurotransmitters and stop feeding and egg-laying activity, and eventually kill the insect.

Inorganics

Sulfur is the oldest known insecticide. Our great grandparents burned sulfur and sulfur candles "for every conceivable purpose, from bedbug fumigation to the cleansing of a house just removed from quarantine of smallpox."[43] It is still used today in integrated pest management programs.

Yet boric acid is perhaps the best known of the inorganics. As a dry powder, it is long lasting and has extended residual effectiveness. It is a stomach poison and also absorbs insect cuticle wax, which dries the insect out and removes its protective outer layer. This same action is performed by the silica gel inorganics.

The Two Keys

- *Active ingredients*
  The active ingredient in an insecticide is what actually kills or repels the insect. This is the ingredient that the registering agencies are most interested in.
- *Inactive ingredients*
  The ingredients listed as "inactive" on insecticide labels are not necessarily nontoxic. They are agents such

as powders that allow the product to be spread more effectively or substances that affect the insecticide's solubility or make it better able to stick to whatever it is aimed at.

The EPA has a great pesticide information Web site for kids (www.epa.gov/opptintr). It includes puzzles, information on what to do in the case of an accident with pesticides, a primer on labels, a test, the ten most-asked questions about pesticides, and this great feature called "The House Tour." The tour begins at a cutaway of a typical two-story house. Click on any room and a close-up of the room appears. In it are several items you can click on, some of them pesticides. For instance, there are six items you can click on in the bedroom, two of which are pesticides (mothballs in the closet and an insect fogger can on the floor). The explanations accompanying the pesticides are not simple one-sentence explanations. They are lengthy descriptions of the form of pesticide you may find (in the case of mothballs, for instance, you may find them as hard balls or in flake form), and what they are, what they are intended to do, what they look and smell like, why you should not disturb them, as well as tips for parents on how to keep them out of kids' reach.

Types of Insecticides Commonly Used for Ant Control
Baits

The little "ant cups" you buy in the grocery, department, or hardware store are baits. These are not traps. They hold a sort of food that attracts the ant to the cup, which is laced with an insecticide. What kinds of foods and which toxins are used depend on the kind of ant. Grease-loving, protein-eating, or sweet-eating ants are all attracted to different kinds of food. And the toxin is tweaked according to the habits and colony structure of the species you're trying to attack.

Bait typically contains a kind of toxin that isn't immediately fatal to the ant, but allows the poisoned colony member enough time to get back to the nest and feed some of the toxin to her colony mates. This way the bait works for more than just the ant that happens to stumble across it. Ideally, one or more of the ants that eat the bait will take it back to the queen, which is the key to eradicating the colony.

"Prebaiting" uses a nontoxic substance to attract the ants—apple mint jelly, for example—and gives the homeowner or pest control expert a chance to observe the ants and locate their nest. The real key to ant control is to find the offending nest and eradicate it.

Desiccants

The function of these compounds is to dry the insect out by attacking its outer shell, thereby killing it. They adhere to the cuticle, scrape a hole, and dry it out. Diatomaceous earth is one example of a desiccant. This dust-like substance can be blown into hard-to-reach wall cracks and crevices—and if kept dry it retains its killing power for years. Especially when carefully applied by a skilled professional, these dusts should not affect humans. If you do choose to blow them in place on your own, use appropriate caution. Use professional-quality safety equipment, including a dust mask and goggles to protect your lungs and eyes.

Silica aerogels are another type of desiccant. These are used when you require quicker action than that provided by a powdered desiccant.

Residual Insecticides

"Residuals" refer to insecticides that have a residual effect. In other words, their effect lasts longer than the immediate impact of the insecticide when it lands on the insect. Residual effects are different for different pesticides. Some have little or no effects—these are the ones you can spray around your home for fleas and then return safely within a couple of hours. The spray kills the existing fleas but has little or no residual ability to kill fleas that come later—such as after new eggs hatch or if an untreated cat walks back in the house, fleas in tow.

Sprays/Fumigants

Insecticides can be delivered in many different ways, and spraying, or fumigating, is one. "Fumigant" typically refers to sprays that are delivered in a gaseous state such as carbon dioxide. Sprays may be mixed with an inactive ingredient that enables the insecticide to be delivered in spray form. This allows the insecticide to be precisely directed at a specific target.

Dusts

Powdered insecticides, referred to as "dusts," are usually used in wall voids and cracks where residual effect is desired but you need to be able to reach the void. Boric acid, diatomaceous earth, pyrethrum, silica aerogel, and sulfur are all dusts. The mineral itself is ground up, or an insecticide is combined with a carrier (the "carrier" transports the insecticide along with it) or adjuvant (the "helper") that can be ground up into dust.

Microencapsulated Formulations

Think of these as time-released medicine. The insecticide is encapsulated in a coating that allows the toxin to slowly release into the pests' environment.

Insect Growth Regulators (IGRs)

These compounds imitate the growth hormone of the juvenile insect, altering it so that the young insect never passes to the adult stage. IGRs are available to control pharaoh ants and fire ants. Although they are slow acting, they leave no residue in the environment and are relatively safe around humans.

Stomach Poisons

Once the ant ingests stomach poisons, it gets sick, and it dies. These are not to be left in areas where children and pets might get to them.

Barrier Treatments

Barrier treatments are sprays and dusts that work to create a barrier, typically a toxic one, around the perimeter of a building. They might be dusts sprinkled into wall voids or sprays spread around foundations. This treatment kills off any insects there at the time and any that might saunter on by after the treatment. Although this kind of treatment probably warrants a toxin with a longer residual effect, the type of chemical used depends on how long lasting it will be when exposed to sunlight, rain, and time.

Repellents/Attractants

Repellents do not typically kill the insect but simply make the insect's target undesirable. Repellents are most often used against biting flies. Attractants are intended to actually draw the insect into a trap or bait with insecticide that it will bring back to the nest.

Integrated Pest Management (IPM)

Integrated pest management brings together many different approaches to tackling your pest problem. Spraying pesticides may be one aspect of your approach, but ultimately it is only *one* approach—not necessarily the first thing you want your pest control expert to try. And when they do turn to pesticides, with an integrated pest management approach, they choose the least amount of it for the job.

Expect the exterminator practicing IPM to assess the situation, complete some identification and nest location work, and then explain his or her plan of attack. IPM means following all the preventive measures recommended. The pest control expert should tell you about baits and other non-widespread pest control treatments, and what options are available besides toxins. They may also describe the level of coverage and control you can expect from certain nontoxic treatments, which may in fact be less than toxic treatments. Will this be enough? Maybe the trade-off is "fewer ants" rather than "no ants," for having significantly less dangerous chemicals tossed around your house. Maybe "fewer ants" will be good enough.

In 1980, the University of California instituted the Statewide Integrated Pest Management Project. This project, supported and encouraged by the state legislature, develops and promotes the use of integrated, ecologically sound pest management practices. Their Web site, www.ipm.ucdavis.edu, provides information about pest control, products, and practices, and has several links such as the one to the EPA's extensive and regularly updated pesticide labeling information site, which can be searched by product number or manufacturer.

Consumer Beware

Ultimately, the pest control practices and pesticides used in and around your home are in your hands. Like everything else you buy, the products and services used to control pests should be bought with the wise eye of a savvy consumer. Practice preventive measures diligently to reduce the incidences of pest problems. Use do-it-yourself pesticides in moderation. If you run across more than a simple ant problem—one or two ants scurrying around your kitchen that a little bait cup eliminates—call in the professionals. They have access to a wider range of products, which may be more toxic, but could also be more effective and they'll be used in smaller quantities than your over-the-counter products. And if all that seems like too much work, read or re-read *Silent Spring*, which should cure anyone of willynilly pesticide use.

7

Natural Ant Control

S tories of home remedies for ant control abound. Almost anything you could think of has been tried on ants to kill or discourage them: talcum powder, boiling water, cloves, chalk, salt. Sprinkled, sprayed, poured, piled in mounds, people try to tempt ants to eat, inhale, climb on, or climb through various products that are repellant or even toxic to the ants if ingested in appropriate quantities.

Many of these are not scientifically tested methods, but represent practical hands-on approaches to meet an ant problem without using chemical pesticides. These methods are your first line of defense against ants. In some cases, they're all you will ever need, depending on the severity of your infestation. If you already have a problem, you may need to go the more toxic route to get you back to ground zero, where you can start again with the less-toxic prevention and control methods described here, which will keep your home to a more tolerable human/ant ratio.

Prevention, Prevention, Prevention

The most effective thing a homeowner can do, either inside or outside, to control ant problems without chemicals is to prevent the ant from becoming a problem in the first place. This can't be emphasized enough—without a population explosion, there is no need for drastic measures.

Furthermore, you need to come to the conclusion that you certainly don't need to eliminate *every* ant within a 250-yard radius of your home. In reasonable numbers, with no enticement to come into your house, ants will go about their business quite unnoticed. And their business is good business—decomposing dead trees, branches, and small animal carcasses, aerating soil, and eating insects that can be peskier than the ants.

But maybe your ants have already gotten out of hand. If so, you need to grit your teeth and call an exterminator to take the edge off the problem, and then go about the business of keeping ants to a bare minimum.

If you haven't taken care of the prevention angle, do that first. Many ideas are outlined in detail in Chapters Four and Five, but here's a quick list of some things to do to get a jump ahead in your non-toxic ant control program:

- Seal all potential entry points in your home, including utility lines, foundations, and door and window frames. This is a tall order but even if you miss a few, it is hugely effective in keeping incoming ants to a bare minimum.
- Take care of all moisture problems. Pay special attention to water lines, air conditioning units, outdoor water spigots, toilets, and areas under sinks. Next to sealing entry points, this is the most important thing you can do. Ants are moisture-seeking insects and are attracted to a water supply as well as the softened wood that surrounds water problems.
- Keep roofs in good repair and regularly clear gutters of debris.
- Properly ventilate attics and bathrooms.

- Mend screens.
- Vacuum regularly.
- Run your dishwasher at least once a day.
- Keep kitchen counters clear of crumbs, drops of liquid, and other ant foods.
- Properly dispose of kitchen garbage, including compost.
- Keep pantry foods in sealed containers.
- Put stored clothing, linens, books, and paper items in sealed storage containers and use deterrents such as cedar to keep pests from using seldom-moved items for nesting.
- Do not leave pet foods sitting out. If your pet is one of those that doesn't eat its entire meal in one sitting, the leftovers may attract ants. You can try setting the pet dish in a pan of water—ants won't swim across the moat to the food.
- Stack firewood away from the house, bringing in only what you will burn soon.
- Never let trees and shrubs touch buildings to make a bridge for ants. Clear overhanging branches from which they can drop from the tree to your house; keep them pruned to a few feet away. This is an often-overlooked but important strategy to keep ants away from buildings.

Repelling

Onions, garlic, and hot peppers can repel existing ant populations or deter infestation in the immediate future. Here is one recipe for an effective deterrent spray:

- Mix ¼ teaspoon cayenne pepper per quart of water, along with a teaspoon of dishwashing liquid (which helps the spray stick to its target). The cayenne pepper can be replaced with the juice of a few crushed hot peppers.

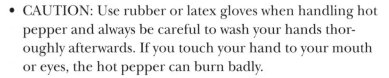

- CAUTION: Use rubber or latex gloves when handling hot pepper and always be careful to wash your hands thoroughly afterwards. If you touch your hand to your mouth or eyes, the hot pepper can burn badly.

If you don't mind that your home has a, shall I say, distinct smell, you can sprinkle powdered garlic around doors, windows, and other ant entry points to repel them.

What's the Hurry?

Horror stories of carpenter ant destruction can lead homeowners to assume that, if they don't call the exterminator the minute they find telltale little sawdust piles and completely soak the house in insecticide within the hour, the place will fall down in a heap by morning. Carpenter ants are capable of extraordinary destruction, but it doesn't happen that fast. You have time to look for the most effective and least toxic method of outwitting them.

Baits

Any baiting substance can either be toxic or not, but its method of use makes it considered a low-toxic type of pest control. The bait is very targeted and will not broadcast in the manner of aerosols and powders. Baits can also be a very effective method of eradicating ants. If the bait is attractive enough, they'll eat it voraciously and take it back to the nest and the queen—within a few weeks, the whole colony will be wiped out.

Not all insects, and not all ants, are easily controlled with baits, though. As researchers at the University of Nebraska found, "in general, ants that eat a wide variety of foods will be less affected because the bait will comprise a smaller proportion of their food."[44] Ants with a sweet tooth tend to be the easiest to control using the baiting method.

Before you put down insect-killing bait, lure the ants to some sweet substance such as jelly. As with all ant tracking, you need to find the best sites for your bait stations. An effective method is to squeeze a ribbon of jelly onto masking tape that's been taped down in suspect areas. (Masking tape will stay in place, but is also easy to remove later.) Check the taped areas in about two hours, counting the number of ants that are visiting each site. If more than ten ants are feeding in any one spot, replace the masking tape with a toxic bait.

Species best controlled by baits include Argentine ants, odorous house ants, small honey ants, pavement ants, little black ants, Pharaoh ants, and big-headed ants.

Boric Acid

The name of this product *sounds* toxic, and used inappropriately and without precautions, it is. But used in recommended ways to control ant populations, it is quite benign and is often categorized as "natural" since it is organic. Boric acid is a white crystalline borate powder made from hydrogen and boron.

Boric acid powder is used to control ants—as well as cockroaches—but it must be carefully applied in a very thin dusting over a target area. Ants avoid piles of the powder. Since it has some residual effect, boric acid powder can also be dusted into wall voids to provide long-lasting control.

Care2 (www.care2.com) was founded in 1998 and expanded from an environmentally friendly greeting card

company to an online community of environmentally con-
scious consumers. Their Web site includes information on
healthy home issues including environmentally friendly
pest control plus eco-news articles covering recent topics,
such as "Florida Citizens Raise Concerns About Pesticide Sprayings to Eradicate Mosquitoes." The site also
has great links, such as the National Coalition Against
the Misuse of Pesticides, and its partners with well-
known groups such as the Nature Conservancy, the National Wildlife Federation, World Wildlife Fund, and others.

Ant Predators

Ant Lions

Ants are a substantial part of the ant lion's diet. The ant lions
themselves, 200 species of which can be found throughout
North America, are innocuous insects. They catch their prey by
digging holes into which ants and other insects fall; the ant lion
then pulls the captured insect below the surface. It is thought,
however, that since ants exist in such large populations, ant lions simply do not eat enough of them to be a significant control.[45]

Birds

Birds are formidable ant predators, perhaps the largest class of
all ant predators. But they also use ants in an interesting behavior referred to as "anting." Some birds will actually apply ants to
their feathers with the presumed benefit of parasitic control. As
they crawl through the bird's feathers, the ants secrete formic
acid or an oily substance from their anal glands.[46]

Other Bugs

Dragonflies and ladybugs are both ant predators. You can purchase predatory bugs at various mail order companies, including:

Beneficial Insectary
9664 Tanqueray Court
Redding, CA 96003
800–477–3715

ARBICO
Arizona Biological
P.O. Box 8910
Tucson, AZ 85738
800–767–2847

Nematodes

Nematodes kill their target insects by entering their bodies and feeding on their blood, which kills the hosts within a day or so. They release a bacterium into the insect's body that preserves the host for as long as the nematode takes to feed and pass through the body, where it searches for the next host. Nematodes can be purchased for distribution in your garden; one such supplier is:

BioLogic
418 Briar Lane
Chambersburg, PA 17201
(717–263–2789)

Purchased nematodes can live for months if kept in the refrigerator. They can be mixed with a bait food, but first test the food to make sure it lures the ants before lacing the food with the nematodes.

Insecticidal Soap

Insecticidal soaps, such as commercially available Safer, create a film that blocks an insect's ability to breathe. You can't, however, just spray your garden; the spray must land directly on the insects. These insecticidal soaps are not entirely benign and can adversely affect the beneficial insects in your garden, so be discriminating in your spraying. Look for the pest insects and target them directly.

You can try making your own soap spray from two to three tablespoons of soap (such as dishwashing liquid) per gallon of water. Avoid soaps with dyes and perfumes that can adversely affect your plants.

Pyrethrins

The pyrethrum flower, a member of the chrysanthemum family, is the source of an important insecticide. Pyrethrin, the active ingredient in the flowers, works by disrupting the normal transmission of nerve impulses, which paralyzes the insect almost immediately. Pyrethrum and its synthetic double, pyrethroid, are considered "safer" because they are not very toxic to mammals. Nonetheless, homeowners should still carefully follow the instructions on the containers. They come in powders, sprays, liquid concentrates, or in "bomb" form.

Natural Diatomaceous Earth

This naturally occurring product has many pest control uses. Mined from fossilized silica shell, diatomaceous earth absorbs the waxy layer on the surface of an insect's skin, drying it out—which, of course, kills it. Since it is "virtually nontoxic to mammals" it is used by some livestock owners to control fly populations.[47] Swimming pool owners will be familiar with diatomaceous earth, although that form is chemically treated with crystalline silica; only natural diatomaceous earth is used for ant control. To apply, sprinkle natural diatomaceous earth in places where ants nest and travel. You can find it at garden centers or at livestock feed and supply stores.

Removal By Hand

One method of pest removal that has been used extensively by organic gardeners for as long as gardening has existed is to simply pick off the pests and crush or otherwise dispose of them. This may be a reasonable method when you need to control the four or five bulging, fat horn worms on your tomato plants, but picking off individual ants, who move pretty quickly when they detect danger, is a bit more difficult.

One way to locate nesting colonies is to use semi-liquid goo such as jam, jelly, or honey to lure them from their nest. Pay attention to where they come from and use a stethoscope to listen for any activity in the walls to confirm your suspicion.

Once you find a carpenter ant nest, it can be effectively removed. Use an industrial-type vacuum cleaner to suck up loose nesting material and stray ants. Depending upon the amount of destruction that has already been inflicted, you may need to also have a skilled carpenter remove and replace, or repair destroyed wood.

Victor's Pest Control supplies nontoxic pest control products including ant bait stations with boric acid and boric acid powders, Poison-Free© Ant and Roach Killer, and

water-based formulas with permethrin as the active ingredient. It also manufactures the Safer line of products such as insecticidal soap. They can be reached
at Woodstream Corp., 69 North Locust Street, Lititz,
PA 17543 (www.victorpest.com).

Good Garden Practices

Ants and other insects in the garden can be kept to a minimum
in large part by using some fairly simple gardening practices:

- *Companion planting:* There are many plants that, when
  planted near each other, protect another plant from insects. For instance, the strong odor of marigolds creates
  an unpleasant environment for many garden insects.
  When interspersed with crops such as tomatoes, they can
  help cut down on insect populations, making an infestation more manageable with friendlier methods. Likewise,
  planting crops in the same family side by side makes both
  crops prone to problems from insects that prey upon that
  particular plant family. Planting all of your squash in one
  area of the garden, for instance, almost ensures that they
  will all have problems with squash beetles.
- *Crop rotation:* To keep garden pests on their toes, don't
  plant the same crop in the same bed of your garden year
  after year after year. Not only will it deplete the soil by
  overburdening much-needed nutrients that the crop
  needs, but it also allows for an unchanging environment
  friendly to pests that prey on that crop. Move crops
  around from year to year, and even intersperse crops
  throughout the garden to further confuse insects when
  they can't find their favorite plant!

- *Fall tilling*: Turn the soil in your garden right before the off season to expose insects and their larvae to the cold air and to predators such as birds.
- *Prompt harvesting*: Don't let ripe produce sit around in your garden providing perfect homes and food sources for pests.

Do not be fooled by insecticidal sprays with nicely perfumed odors! Pleasant-smelling or not, they are still highly toxic. Keep them away from children and pets.

Unconventional Treatments

Electricity

The Electrogun was invented by Dr. L. G. Lawrence. Although it is not understood exactly how the electrical gun kills insects when directed into their nests at low energy and high frequency, that's exactly what happens. This method is completely harmless to humans because it emits no harmful radiation or any residue. The Electrogun is probably best left to the experts, however, since it requires some experience and skill to operate effectively.

Heat

Much like electricity, heat has proven to be another effective carpenter ant control method with no side effects or residual impact. Scientists Charles Forbes and Walter Eberling, who developed this treatment, found that insects could be killed if the temperature where they are located is raised to 120 degrees or higher. Done properly and with the appropriate precautions, this treatment kills insects without damaging your home.

Dogs

According to *Common-Sense Pest Control*, "Hiring a company that uses termite-detecting dogs will likely produce superior results. Like their bomb- and narcotics-detecting counterparts, these dogs, usually beagles, are specially trained to smell wood-damaging insects."[48] Not only can canines wiggle into spaces humans can't reach, they're also insured against errors. Furthermore, if a claim is made against the guarantee issued by a pest control company, a dog-assisted inspection is admissible in court.

Unfortunately, a dog inspection also means a higher cost, but the cost is well justified. The inspection is much more thorough, and infestation sites are pinpointed. So, instead of treating an entire house, a dog-led detail will concentrate your treatment strictly on the infestation site, which can save you much time and money.

Other General Treatments

- Always scrub with detergent any surfaces where you find ants making their way to a food source. This removes the pheromone trails they have established to trace their way back to your kitchen or pantry.
- If your pet is one of those that doesn't finish a bowl of food in one sitting, eating off and on all day long, and the pet's dish is attracting ants, set the dish in a pan of water such as an old pie plate. The ants won't swim over to the bowl.
- Entry points can be blocked with duct tape or petroleum jelly.

- Extreme infestations call for extreme measures. Include in your line of attack things like rinsing meat wrappers and other food wrapping before putting them in the trash.
- Pour boiling water into an ant nest for a direct means of eliminating an entire nest. For fire ant control, find the nest and plan to use approximately three gallons of boiling water per nest mound. In order to be sure you're getting to as many ants as possible, pick a sunny, cool day when the ants will be near the nest's surface. Slowly pour the water onto the nest mound. Although perhaps a cruel method of elimination, boiling water is about as non-toxic as you can get.
- Ant colonies, once found in houses, can be successfully vacuumed up. But don't pull the Hoover out of the closet for this! It's best left to pest control experts who have access to commercial-strength vacuums that are made solely for this purpose.

Pest Control Experts and Non-Toxic Treatments

If you choose to use a pest control company to take care of your problem for you, but one of your major concerns is the level of toxins they'll use around your home, ask some questions before hiring a company. Find out what their basic approach and attitude is—if you know what kind of pests you need to tackle, ask about how they will control those pests specifically.

Intricate state and federal regulations exist to control the use of pesticides. The company, your local extension service, health and human services department, or agricultural agency should be able to provide you with literature that explains the products the company may use. If an exterminator is unwilling to provide you with this information, find another exterminator.

Find out how their ongoing service operates. Perhaps you have a huge carpenter ant problem and the best way to get rid of them is to use toxins. The pest control experts come and exterminate them and you perform all the appropriate sealing, pruning, and preventive measures. Now what? If you sign on with the company for monthly or twice-monthly visits, will they simply spray and call it a day? Or will they actually monitor the situation, spraying only when necessary? Better yet, after the initial treatment, will they have a less-toxic program of ongoing control? Are they willing and advanced enough to try the newest, least-toxic products and measures?

The company you speak with should also be willing to discuss alternative pest control methods with authority and enthusiasm. You should feel like your concerns are respected and not dismissed as silly or unimportant. It's your house, your environment, and your decision who will treat your home.

The Long Haul

Keep in mind that less-toxic pest control methods almost inevitably mean shorter effectiveness. The very nature of the less toxic substances is that they break down relatively quickly when exposed to air, sunshine, heat, or rain. You will need to be diligent about preventive measures and about continuing to apply non-toxic controls.

Also, remember that just because one product or substance is less toxic than another, it is still capable of killing not just the target pest, but other insects as well, both pestiferous and beneficial. And diligently keep all such products out of the reach of children and pets.

8

Other Pesty Insects

We share our world with lots of insects. Unfortunately, we also share our houses, yards, and gardens with lots of insects, sometimes unbeknownst to us human inhabitants. For the most part, these insects aren't cause for much alarm. Unless they become so large in number that they are scurrying all over our furniture or attacking us the minute we step out the door, we really should be able to co-exist amicably.

But we don't usually relish the thought of sharing our homes and yards with insects. Spiders in the corner, wasps in the garage, ants in the kitchen, bees under the eaves, and silverfish in the tub are a signal to take up arms. We smash, spray, and sometimes even flush our way to a bug-free environment.

Here's some information on some of the more common insects we encounter in our homes—and the lowdown on what should cause us to act and when, as well as which bugs are simply not a problem and don't require any overreaction.

Aphids

Since aphids are so important to ants, and the two have such a symbiotic relationship, they have been discussed at length in at least several other places in this book. These insects damage and weaken plants by sucking juices from the leaves. They are protected by many species of ants, which not only drive off aphid predators but also even carry them to safer ground when the aphids are threatened. Ants do this gladly in exchange for the precious honeydew aphids produce and that ants thrive on.

If you have an aphid infestation, assume ants are somewhere around as well. Be careful not to infest your garden with aphids by bringing in plants from outside with aphids on them. Inspect all new plants carefully and get rid of aphids before introducing the new plant to your garden.

Aphids can be easily but somewhat tediously (depending on the size of your garden) removed from plants by spraying them with soapy water and knocking the insects off the host plant. They are thought not to climb back up onto the plant.

Deter aphid development by deeply tilling the soil in the fall or several times in the spring, exposing their larvae to the elements before planting.

Bees

Bees are rarely pests although many people consider even one bee to present a problem. They belong to the same order as ants and wasps, Hymenoptera, and hold a very important place in agriculture as the main pollination vehicle of plants. Most bees live solitary lives, but honeybees are well known for their complex societies. Honeybees are often domesticated and as well as providing a necessary pollination service, they are sources of wax and honey.

Bees are very susceptible to pesticides and any pesticide use should carefully account for its impact on bee populations.

Carpenter bees have developed more of a reputation as pests than they deserve. They are nowhere near as destructive as carpenter ants. As for houses, they tend to view unpainted or weathered wood as a great place to rear young, but carpenter bees are loners and will not build nests to house colonies. They are very slow to work on wood structures and never reach the destructive proportions of termites and carpenter ants. Unfortunately, their wood-boring activity is sometimes expanded by woodpeckers, making the bees unwitting accomplices to structural damage.

Although we tend to think of all bees as stinging insects just waiting for a human victim, only the female carpenter bee is capable of stinging, and she does it only rarely. The males are more territorial and give a good show when disturbed by humans, but the show is a bluff—stingless, they can do no harm.

There are seven species of carpenter bees ranging widely across the entire U.S. They do resemble bumblebees, but if you can get close enough, you can distinguish them from bumblebees by their bare shiny top abdomen areas. If you see these large bees hovering near your house, look for other signs of infestation. Round holes, about one to two inches in circumference, in siding or trim and sawdust-like piles below their work areas will give them away.

Clothes Moths

Clothes moths are described in the *NPCA Field Guide to Structural Pests* as two types: casemaking and webbing clothes moths. It is the webbing clothes moth that we encounter most often as pests. The larvae of the webbing clothes moth builds a silk covering around itself and the area it's feeding on. You will find these silky larvae in areas of clothing—typically stored clothing that goes undisturbed for long periods of time—in hidden spots like under collars and cuffs. They are after the keratin in animal products, so do not tend to feed on straight synthetic fibers or fabrics that are made from vegetable products. The adults do not feed.

Whereas most moths are attracted to light, as anyone who has sat on a porch in the summer with the light on knows, webbing clothes moths avoid light and will scamper when exposed. Interestingly, these moths do not fly well, preferring to run instead. Males can fly a little better than females, but they won't win any Insect Olympic gold medals.

To deter clothes moths, do not store clothing made from fabrics that they're attracted to without first cleaning it. Unable to survive solely on unprocessed wool, the moth seeks out stains as added nutritional supplements—be they food, beverage, sweat, or urine. Cedar will repel but not kill the moths. After cleaning, the next most important step you can take to protect stored clothes is to seal them in mothproof storage containers, such as plastic storage bins, garbage bags, or sealed plastic bags.

Climate control can also help since the moths thrive in humidity and cannot withstand long periods of temperatures higher than 100 degrees Fahrenheit. Sticky tape and trap systems are also available. Clothes moths will also respond to many pesticides, and a pest control expert can help you rid them from your house.

Cockroaches

Ah, the cockroach. Famous long before Kafka's *Metamorphosis*, this ancient creature has roamed the earth almost since the beginning of time. They were fully evolved nearly from the start around 400 million years ago. Several thousand species exist with several thousand more believed to yet be identified. There are several dozen in the U.S. with the most common pests being the American, brownbanded, German, oriental, and smoky-brown. Ironically, the German cockroach is the most common pest in the U.S. But Australian cockroaches are prevalent in the South, since they cannot tolerate colder climates.

Sanitation is the key to cockroach prevention. Their food sources *must* be removed. These insects have had a long history of survival and once entrenched, they are hard to get rid of without insecticides. They're shy creatures that like to hide in tiny cracks and crevices so baits need to be strategically placed in appropriate areas. Sealing their hiding places can be a good preventive measure. Cockroaches are nocturnal, but if the infestation is extensive, they may be seen in daylight hours.

If you live in a multi-unit building, it may be hard to rid the entire building of roaches if everyone does not practice meticulous sanitation. If just one unit manages to control roaches, they'll simply move on to overpopulate another unit.

Fleas

There are cat fleas, dog fleas, and human fleas. The most common of the three is the cat flea, although it is by no means exclusive to cats. The cat flea (*Ctenocephalides felis*) feeds on many other kinds of mammals as well, and can transmit organisms such as the bacteria that causes bubonic plague. They can also cause serious allergic reactions in animals and humans who are susceptible to them, and the flea can host a tapeworm, which can be transmitted to dogs, cats, and humans. These are nasty pests!

Fleas, like ants, pass through the four developmental stages of egg, larva, pupa, and adult. They thrive in warm, but not hot, and humid conditions—dryness is fatal to the flea. The unique and important fact to know about the flea is that its larvae can live for months without feeding. So, when a human or pet comes home from a vacation, newly hatched fleas, and any adults who have gone for a while without a blood meal, will eagerly attack you upon your return.

Two things can significantly repress the flea population in your home:

1. Vacuum regularly and thoroughly to pick up fleas emerging from their various stages and to remove the eggs from corners where the adults like to deposit them.

2. Groom your pets with a flea comb to keep as many fleas as possible off of them as well as to keep track of the level of flea infestation your pet may be experiencing (drown the fleas you comb out in warm soapy water).

There are a few other things you should do. Designate a specific area or bed for your pet to sleep in that is easy to regularly clean. An occasional soapy warm dog bath (you can attempt a cat bath if you want, but I've never been quite game enough for that) will kill lots of fleas even without requiring "flea shampoos." If a dog's flea problem is extensive, some mild flea shampoos will treat it effectively. Be very careful with your pets when using these shampoos, though—for example, don't interchange dog and cat shampoos. Flea collars, daily brewer's yeast tablets or powder, and cedar bedding are just a few of the possibilities for keeping your pets' flea population to a minimum.

Extreme flea infestations will need professional extermination services, which may include insecticides, heat treatments, freezing, steaming, and other approaches. Because of the various stages of the flea's development, you will need to pre-clean your house before treatment. Expect a need for re-treatment in around three weeks, however, to get all the newly hatched larvae.

Fruit Flies

Let a few bananas, apples, tomatoes, or even potatoes get a little ripe and in no time your kitchen will be host to dozens of teeny little *Drosophila*, the common small fruit fly (not to be confused with the more famous agricultural pest, the Mediterranean fruit fly, *Ceratitis capitata*). They're mostly nuisance pests, but according to the *NPCA Field Guide to Structural Pests*, the fruit fly can act as an intermediate host to certain diseases. Fruit flies are such simple and quickly reproducing creatures that *Drosphila melanogaster* is used extensively in genetics research.

This rapid growth and prolific reproduction make fruit flies such pests. The eggs laid by the adult hatch in just over a day. The entire maturation process from egg to adult takes well under two weeks, and mature adults can mate within two days of maturation.

To avoid a fruit fly population explosion, keep areas to which they may be attracted clean and free of possible yeast-producing food products. Once fruit has started to decay, they are no longer interested; it is the initial fermentation phase that attracts the fruit fly. Any attempt to eradicate them will be short-lived without careful sanitation.

Houseflies

Like many insects found in and around our homes, houseflies are not only nuisance pests but they're also disease-carriers. Although perhaps not commonly transmitted in most of the U.S., the housefly (*Musca domestica*) can carry malaria, trypanosomiasis (the sleeping sickness), and typhoid fever. Their larval stage is what we commonly refer to as maggots. The maggot stage can last for a long time, even as long as two years, although the housefly completes its entire metamorphosis in as little as just over a week.

Houseflies, part of the grouping of pests known as "filth flies," are attracted to garbage. Period. Besides human waste, they are also attracted to pet droppings, so be sure to take the time to clean up after your dogs and cats. In rural areas, if you keep any kind of livestock be sure to pick up after them at least daily. In some urban areas, local stables or dog kennels can contribute to the problem, but human sanitation is really the most significant factor as to whether or not houseflies become huge pests.

Pesticides are not a good control method for houseflies. Prevention is far more logical and effective. Keep your garbage cans clean, use tightly sealed garbage bags, get your trash out of your house and off your premises on a regular basis, and you'll go far in controlling the house fly population. Also, be sure screens on doors and windows are tight and in good repair. Unfortunately, you'll need to hope your neighbors are being just as neat because, of course, flies fly!

The housefly is gray in color and, if you get up close and personal, you will see four stripes on the thorax. There are many other kinds of flies similar to the housefly—the vinegar fly, the stable fly, and the drone fly to name just a few.

Lice

Head lice are still a more common problem in the U.S. than one might imagine, but body lice are rare. The good news is that body lice pose a greater health threat, the bad news is that head lice are difficult to get rid of. Lice are also becoming resistant to the insecticides once commonly used to manage head lice infestations. These products are quite hazardous, too.

Head lice are most prevalent among school-age children, which makes the managing of them a serious issue facing schools worldwide. Millions of children are treated in the U.S. every year.

Although head lice cannot fly or jump, they can walk pretty quickly from one host to another if, say, an infected child sits or sleeps near another child for any length of time. The adult lice and eggs can transfer from one person to another via any exchange of clothing, especially hats and scarves, as well as hairbrushes, towels, pillows, and even furniture.

Powderpost Beetles

When I bought a 200-year-old home and followed the home inspector around for the pre-purchase inspection, I was able to see firsthand the evidence left behind by these almost invisible little wood-boring beetles. Luckily, the early settlers who built houses like mine used timbers so huge that, as the inspector explained to me, the beams could be reduced to a third their size and still exceed current standards.

Eleven species of powderpost beetles are found throughout the U.S. The two identified by the NPCA as the most damaging in this country are the southern lyctus beetle (*Lyctus planicollis*) and the velvety powderpost beetle (*Trogoxylon parallelopipedum*).

The powderpost beetle does its damage at the larval stage. The female taste tests the wood, looking for high starch content. When she finds a particularly tasty site, which is typically in more porous woods such as oak, hickory, and ash, she lays two to three dozen eggs, which hatch into larvae that remain in the wood, boring their trademark holes and tunnels, usually until the following spring. The rapidity of their development depends on the wood's starch content, and the humidity level of the environment. They need a starch content of higher than three percent and moisture levels ideally between ten and twenty percent.

Signs of powderpost beetle damage are the holes and tunnels, as well as a fine powder of wood dust along the tunnels and exit holes. They only infest untreated wood, never wood that has been varnished or stained. Generally, they don't fly, but after emerging as adults they lay eggs in the wood from which they've emerged.

Silverfish

Silverfish (*Lepisma saccharina*) are nocturnal insects that thrive in moist environments. They are grayish-silver to green in color and their sectioned carrot-shaped bodies resemble miniature collapsible cups. They feed on starch, so are often found around books, where they feast on the starchy substances in the books' binding. They also eat wallpaper paste. They are biologically and ecologically similar to the mottled black and white "firebrat," which also thrives in moist environments and feeds on starch. Between the two, there are almost 350 species in the U.S.

You won't see silverfish often, since they're quite elusive, but if they get into your bathtub or sink, they can't climb out. Females lay a couple of eggs a day that take anywhere from a few months to a couple of years to develop into adults, depending on conditions. The average lifespan of the adult is three years.

According to the *NPCA Field Guide to Structural Pests*, the fourlined silverfish can be commonly found outdoors in temperate climates in mulch and in the bark of California's eucalyptus trees.

Termites

Ah, behold the termite. This is the third in the infamous trio of home pest insects, the other two being carpenter ants and cockroaches. Termites are pale in color and are sometimes called "white ants." But they actually are quite different from ants, the first difference being their body shape. Ants belong to a completely different order almost by virtue of their waist-line—termites, after all, have no waist. But they also have straight little antennae while ants' antennae are jointed.

Also social insects, termites have some distinctions from ants in that regard as well. While an ant's sex determines its caste,

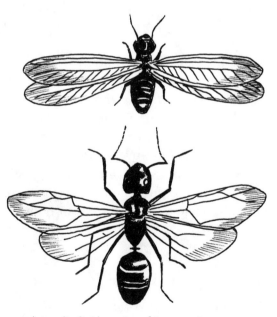

A termite (top) compared to an ant.

the different castes of the termite colony include both males and females. A colony of termites can contain millions of individuals. They have a simple metamorphosis, from egg to nymph to adult. Of the more than 2,000 species of termites found in the world, only forty-one can be found in North America.

Termites serve a very useful purpose in the environment and have been around over 250 million years to prove it. There are three categories of termite and it is essential to identify the category—subterranean, drywood, or dampwood—in order to effectively control a termite problem in a structure.

Subterranean termites build distinctive tunnels along foundations or wherever they are invading susceptible wood in order to protect themselves from predators and from drying out. They have a high need for moisture while drywood termites do not, allowing them to attack wood that is not near a moisture source.

If you wait to see swarming termites before worrying about their presence in your home, you are inviting damage. Monitor your home regularly for termites and any wood-damaging insects. Inspect the foundations for termite evidence: tunnels, holes in punky wood, and discarded fecal matter, wings, and other debris. The list of preventive measures in Chapter Four is similar to what will prevent termite infestations. Pesticides, heat, and electricity are among the options a pest control company will consider to eliminate termites from your home.

Ticks

Outwitting Ticks will provide you with the details you need to know about this important pest species.[49] Tiny little deer ticks are known to spread the relatively new and debilitating Lyme disease to both humans and pets. These round, hard-bodied bloodsuckers look like little dots with legs and mandibles, and are to be avoided. At least three seasons of the year, they wait in grass and on shrubs for a warm-blooded host to come along and sweep them off their feet. According to the *NPCA Field Guide to Structural Pests*, deer ticks live on white-tailed deer in the winter and lay as many as 3,000 eggs when they drop off in the spring.

To reduce tick populations around your home, keep grass and shrubs cut low and remove woodpiles and other debris that attract the white-footed mice on which the tick nymphs nest.

You can soak yourself with insecticides to repel them, or you can protect yourself with appropriate clothing when walking in the woods. To be able to readily see ticks on you and to keep them off your skin, wear light-colored, long-sleeved shirts and long pants, and tuck your pants into light-colored socks. Check yourself and your pets thoroughly before going into your house. Do not touch ticks with your hands; remove ticks with tweezers and dispose of them (we burn them in a special ashtray since it's almost impossible to crush their hard bodies).

Wasps

Bees and wasps are, for the most part, beneficial insects. Some people, however, are extremely allergic to them and a few dozen deaths from wasp and bee stings occur in the U.S. each year. They can become pests when they accumulate in large numbers in areas frequented by humans.

The common yellow jacket is a scavenger—the pesty wasp that arrives at the same time as your *al fresco* lunch on lovely warm fall days. It's primarily attracted to the food, but it can also be drawn to your perfume, cologne, hair spray, and shaving lotion, as well as brightly colored clothing. As pesty as yellow jackets may be, they are also very beneficial, since they eat many pest insects.

Wasps that make ground nests swarm ferociously when disturbed. Be aware of where you are walking and stick to well-worn paths. Don't sit down on the ground outdoors without first checking carefully for wasp activity indicative of a nest entrance. If you find ground nests near your home, you can eradicate them, or better yet mark them, so you and your family can allow these beneficial insects to do their thing while you leave them in peace. Keep garbage carefully wrapped in plastic bags and in tightly closed trashcans to reduce wasps' and bees' interest in these food sources, especially yellow jackets.

Mud daubers are social wasps that live in mud nests. They have bright yellow markings and a sting like a hot match head. (I know, as does a horse I once had who we discovered had a mud dauber family in her stall, which, needless to say, she was not happy about!) Mud daubers prey on spiders, so if you find a mud dauber nest, you can decide which you like the least.

Wasps nesting on your home are probably best eradicated; if you have one paper wasp nest to knock down or spray, do this in the evening when the nest is mostly inactive. If your infestation is large, you are probably better off hiring a professional who knows exactly how to attack the situation and has access to the best kind of protective gear.

There Are Plenty More

These are really just the tip of the pest insect iceberg. Typically, as with outwitting ants, the most important thing you can do is practice good sanitation when it comes to garbage and compost, along with practicing good housecleaning habits such as regular vacuuming, keeping foodstuffs in sealed containers, wiping counters, and sweeping floors. And then give yourself over to the fact that a world without any insects would not only be boring but probably also could never exist. Do what you can to keep the populations to a minimum, then get out a magnifying glass and observe the rest!

Conclusion

After researching ants for this book, I have more admiration for them than ever. I believe, as with all animals humans consider pests, it is partly our responsibility to keep them at bay. In other words, it seems unfair to keep a filthy, unmaintained home that encourages ant populations only to then kill them when they try to take advantage of an environment so conducive to their needs. If you keep your home environment unappealing they won't become pests in the first place; you will save yourself time and money, and you will save the world from further pesticide use that could have been avoided.

All that said, ants haven't been around millions of years for no reason—they are good adaptors and they can become household pests despite your best efforts to keep them out. If the weather turns unfavorable, ant colonies will turn to the best environment for their survival, which often includes buildings occupied by humans.

Do the best you can and remember: Ants happen.

Notes

Chapter 1: The History and Folklore of the Ant

1. Caryl P. Haskins, *Of Ants and Men* (New York: Prentice Hall, 1939), 9.
2. Haskins, 10.
3. Peter Farb, *The Insects* (New York: Time-Life, 1962), 170.
4. Haskins, 23.
5. Haskins, 5.
6. Timothy C. Lockley, "Imported Fire Ants," <http://ipm world.upm.edu/chapters/lockley.htm>.
7. Joshua Tompkins, "Empire of the Ants," *Los Angeles Times Magazine* (February 2001): 66.
8. William Olkowski, Sheila Daar, and Helga Olkowski, *Common-Sense Pest Control* (Newport, CT: Taunton Press, 1991), 440.

Chapter 2: Species: The Few That Torment Us and Some That Don't

9. Thompkins, 66.
10 "Fire ants" FAQ sheet, <http://www.antcolony.org>.
11. "Fireants," Colorado State University, <http://www.colostate.edu>.

12. Bert Hölldobler and Edward O. Wilson, *Journey to the Ants* (Cambridge, MA: Belknap Press, 1994), 112.

13. Hölldobler and Wilson, 175–76.

Chapter 3: Anatomy and Behavior

14. Edward O. Wilson, *In Search of Nature* (Washington, D.C.: Island Press, 1996), 47.

15. John H. Sudd, *An Introduction to the Behaviours of Ants* (London: Edward Arnold, 1967), 13.

16. Wilson, 68–69

17. William Morton Wheeler, *Ants: Their Structure, Development, and Behavior* (New York: Columbia, 1913), 69.

18. Wheeler, 186.

19. Sudd, 9.

20. Wilson, 63.

21. S. Milius, "To Save Gardens, Ants Rush to Whack Weeds." *Science News* (19 May 2000): n.p.

22. Wheeler, 186.

23. Augustus Forel, quoted in Farb, 168.

24. Sudd, 128.

25. Hölldobler and Wilson, 49–50.

26. Farb, 125.

27. *Science Weekly* (27 August 1999): n.p.

28. *USNews* (27 July 1998): n.p.

29. *Science News* (5 February 2000): n.p.

30. Hölldobler and Wilson, plate caption, 196g.

Chapter 4: Ants in the House

31. Libby Copeland, "Ants, Ants Everywhere," *Washington Post* (8 August 1999): n.p.

32. Eric H. Smith and Richard C. Whitman, *NPCA Field Guide to Structural Pests* (NPCA, 1992).

33. Smith and Whitman.

34. Smith and Whitman.

35. Smith and Whitman.

36. Smith and Whitman.

Chapter 5: Ants in the Yard and Garden

37. Copeland, n.p.

38. Sally Jean Cunningham, *Great Garden Companions* (Emmaus, PA: Rodale Press, 1998).

39. "Fire ants" FAQ sheet, <http://www.antcolony.org>.

Chapter 6: Pesticides and Chemicals

40. George W. Ware, "An Introduction to Insecticides," Paper (December, 1999).

41. Ware.

42. Ware.

43. Ware.

Chapter 7: Natural Ant Control

44. Barb Ogg, *Ant Baits* (University of Nebraska Cooperative Extension Fact sheet).

45. "Naughty or Nice? Ant Lions," *Organic Gardening* (April 1997): 22.

46. Eldon D. Greij, "Anting," *Birder's World* 11 (August 1997): 70.

47. Olkowski et al., 111.

48. Olkowski et al., 436.

Chapter 8: Other Pesty Insects

49. Susan Carol Hauser, *Outwitting Ticks* (New York: Lyons Press, 2001).

Bibliography

Carson, Rachel. *Silent Spring*. Greenwich, CT: Fawcett, 1962.

Cohen, Nancy E. "On the Trail of Ants' Fancy Footwork." *Science News*, 10 January 1998.

Copeland, Libby. "Ants, Ants Everywhere: Not a Drop to Drink Outside, So Pests Come In from Drought." *The Washington Post*, Prince William Extra, 29 August 1999.

Cunningham, Sally Jean. *Great Garden Companions*. Emmaus, PA: Rodale Press, 1998.

Farb, Peter. *The Insects*. New York: Time-Life, 1962.

"*Fireants.*" Fact sheet. Colorado State University Web site <www.colostate.edu>.

"*Fire Ants.*" FAQ Sheet, <www.antcolony.org>.

Greij, Eldon D. "Anting." *Birder's World* 11, August 1997: 70.

Haskins, Caryl P. Ph.D. *Of Ants and Men*. New York: Prentice-Hall, 1939.

Hölldobler, Bert, and Edward O. Wilson. *Journey to the Ants*. Cambridge, Mass: Belknap Press, 1994.

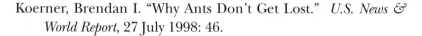

Koerner, Brendan I. "Why Ants Don't Get Lost." *U.S. News & World Report,* 27 July 1998: 46.

Levi, Herbert W. *Spiders and Their Kin.* New York: St. Martin's, 1996.

Lockley, Timothy C. "Imported Fire Ants." <http://ipmworld. upm.edu/chapters/lockley.htm>.

Milius, S. "To Save Gardens, Ants Rush to Whack Weeds." *Science News,* 19 May 2000.

Milius, Susan. "When Ants Squeak." *Science News,* 5 February 2000.

"Naughty? Nice? Or Neutral? Ant Lions." *Organic Gardening.* April 1997: 22.

Ogg, Barb. *Ant Baits: A Least Toxic Control.* University of Nebraska Cooperative Extension Factsheet: 267–95.

Olkowski, William, Sheila Daar, and Helga Olkowski. *Commonsense Pest Control.* Newport, CT: Taunton Press: 1991.

Roberts, Tom. *100% Natural Organic Pest Control for Home and Garden.* TN: Book Publishing Company, 1998.

Sisson, Robert F. "At Home with the Bulldog Ant." *National Geographic,* July 1974.

Smith, Eric H., and Richard C. Whitman. *NPCA Field Guide to Structural Pests.* NPCA, 1992.

Sudd, John H., Ph.D. *An Introduction to the Behaviour of Ants.* London: Edward Arnold Publishers, 1967.

Tompkins, Joshua. "Empire of the Ants." *Los Angeles Times Magazine,* February 2001

Ware, George W. "An Introduction to Insecticides." Paper, December 1999.

Wheeler, William Morton, PhD. *Ants: Their Structure, Development, and Behavior.* New York: Columbia University Press, 1913.

Wilson, Edward O. *In Search of Nature.* Washington, D.C.: Island Press, 1996.

Glossary

Axonic poison:
A pesticide (for example, DDT, some pyrethroids, and pyrethrum) that affects the electrical impulse transmission along the axons, the long extensions of the neuron cell.

Callow:
An ant that has just emerged from the pupa.

Crop:
The stomach used to store food that is shared with other ants.

Desiccation:
Drying out; some pesticides cause insects to dry out, which kills them.

Ethology:
The study of behavior under natural conditions

Eusocial:
Truly social.

Gaster:
Back section of the abdomen.

Majors:
Large soldiers.

Mandibles:
Strong tong-like jaws on either side of the mouth.

Maxillae:
Small jaws that chew food.

Medias:
Intermediate-sized workers.

Metamorphosis:
The changes in form during the ant's four-stage life cycle, from egg to adult.

Minors:
Small-sized workers.

Ocelli:
Simple eyes found on some ants on the top of the head.

Pedicel:
The segment of the ant's body between the thorax and the abdomen.

Pheromone:
The chemical scent that leaves a trail from the food source to the nest that is recognized by all members of a colony.

Polymorphism:
Having a caste system where members of a species each specialize in a different social function.

Population biology:
The study of entire populations of organisms using mathematical models as well as field study and lab research.

Strigil:
The middle joint of each front leg. The strigil is used extensively in cleaning dirt from antennae and other legs.

Trophobiosis:
The symbiotic relationship of one species providing another with nourishment in exchange for protection; for example, ants and aphids.

Trophyllaxis:
Regurgitating food into another's mouth.

Significant Entomologists

The study of ants, known as myrmecology, was not officially recognized as a branch of entomology until 1908. But that didn't seem to worry scientists much; regardless of lacking a stamp of scientific authenticity, they studied the ant anyway. It wasn't until the 1960s and 1970s, however, that a revolution in biology moved ant study forward exponentially.

Some of the most well known entomologists and naturalists devoted much of their research and fascination to myrmecology, whether so-named or not.

- **Charles Darwin** (1809–1882): Although not known to history in general for his ant studies, British naturalist Darwin was said to be very interested in ants. Their characteristic of having sterile workers was counter to his evolutionary theory of natural selection and survival of the fittest since the "fittest" in the case of ants (the female workers) couldn't reproduce. The sacrificial nature of individual ants for the superorganism of the colony fit in quite well, however.
- **Auguste Forel** (1841–1912): This Swiss myrmecologist, wrote *Fourmis de la Suisse* early in his more than fifty-year

career of investigating the taxonomy and social life of ants.

- **William D. Hamilton** (1936–2000): British entomologist and geneticist Hamilton was responsible for the theory that the sex of bees, ants, and wasps is determined by "haplodiploidy"—that fertilized eggs become females and unfertilized eggs become males.
- **Bert Hölldobler** (1936–   ): German entomologist and Professor at the University of Wurzberg, Hölldobler co-authored (with Edward O. Wilson) the Pulitzer Prize-winning monograph *The Ants*.
- **William M. Mann** (1886–1960): Myrmecologist Mann was also a former director of the National Museum of Natural History in Washington, D.C.
- **Carl Rettenmeyer** (1931–   ): An American entomologist, Rettenmeyer discovered the species of army ant that serves as host to the macrochelid mite. The mite attaches itself to the foot of the ant, from which it sucks blood for sustenance while the ant spends its life going about its business as if the mite was just a natural extension of its foot.
- **William Morton Wheeler** (1865–1937): America's leading myrmecologist left no facet of myrmecology unexamined. In 1925, Wheeler pointed out that ants use the simplest of nesting materials (dirt for the most part), which probably contributed to their lengthy survival.
- **Edward O. Wilson** (1929–   ): Contemporary American entomologist and Harvard professor, Wilson co-authored (with Bert Hölldobler) the Pulitzer Prize-winning monograph *The Ants*.

Index

Trogoxylon parallelopipedum
    velvety powderpost beetle, 131
Tropical fire ant *(Solenopsis geminata),* 16
Two-node pedicel, 32

U
Uncle Milton ant farms, 27
Unconventional treatments, 119–120
Utility lines
    ant entry points, 52

V
Vacuum
    ant colonies, 121
    repress flea population, 128
Velvety powderpost beetle *(Trogoxylon parallelopipedum),* 131
Velvety tree ants *(Liometopum occidentale),* 22
    in yard and garden, 89
Victor's Pest Control, 117–118
    web site, 118

W
Wall-nesting. *See also* Nests
    group list, 12
Wasps, 6, 135–136
Waste
    keeping ants out, 56
Water, 43
    lines
        ant entry points, 52

outdoor spigots
    appealing to ants, 54
Water-seeking missiles, 53
Weather and climate conditions
    drive ants into house, 78
Weaver ant, 47
Web sites
    ant colonies, 10
    Care2, 113
    EPA, 103
    Extension Toxicology Network, 95
    IPM, 108
    National Pesticide Information Center, 99
    Victor's Pest Control, 118
Wheeler, William Morton, 35, 38, 45
White, E. B., 91
Wilson, Edward O., 18, 31, 43, 49
Windows
    ant entry points, 52
Winged males, 39
Wings, 31–32
Wood ant *(Formica polyctena),* 48
Wood-damaging insects, 134
Workers, 39

Y
Yard and garden
    ants, 77–90
Yarrow, 84
Yellow jacket, 135